Incredible Stories of Miracles at the Door

Changing Lives While Sharing the Good News

Devon L. Roberts

TEACH Services, Inc.
P U B L I S H I N G
www.TEACHServices.com • (800) 367-1844

World rights reserved. This book or any portion thereof may not be copied or reproduced in any form or manner whatever, except as provided by law, without the written permission of the publisher, except by a reviewer who may quote brief passages in a review.

The author assumes full responsibility for the accuracy of all facts and quotations as cited in this book. The opinions expressed in this book are the author's personal views and interpretations, and do not necessarily reflect those of the publisher.

This book is provided with the understanding that the publisher is not engaged in giving spiritual, legal, medical, or other professional advice. If authoritative advice is needed, the reader should seek the counsel of a competent professional.

Copyright © 2023 Devon L. Roberts
Copyright © 2023 TEACH Services, Inc.
ISBN-13: 978-1-4796-1652-7 (Paperback)
ISBN-13: 978-1-4796-1653-4 (ePub)
Library of Congress Control Number: 2023911962

Unless otherwise indicated, all Scripture quotations are taken from the King James Version.

www.TEACHServices.com • (800) 367-1844

Dedication

This book is dedicated to my darling wife, Cynthia, the queen of my heart and the jewel in my crown. I want to thank her for never giving up on me. For the past twenty plus years, she has been relentless in her suggestion for me to put my experiences in a book. Now by God's grace, her persistent efforts have prevailed.

To my wonderful son, Daniel, for his thoughtfulness, alacrity, and willingness to help whenever he was called upon.

To my precious daughter, Khalilah, whose spirit of love overshadowed her disabilities and gave me the inspiration and incentive to write.

To the memory of my loving mother, Ada, and father, Herman, with the blessed hope of reuniting with them soon when they shall rise in the first resurrection.

TABLE OF CONTENTS

Acknowledgments	vii
Introduction	9
Chapter One: The First Rainy-Day Miracle at the Last Door	13
Chapter Two: The Second Rainy-Day Miracle at the Last Door	17
Chapter Three: The Third Rainy-day Miracle at the Last Door	25
Chapter Four: The Fourth Miracle at the Last Door	29
Chapter Five: A Miracle at My Work Room Door	33
Chapter Six: Another Miracle at My Work Room Door	37
Chapter Seven: The Works of Fallen Angels Continue	41
Chapter Eight: Another Remarkable Miracle at My Work Room Door	49
Chapter Nine: Are You an Angel?	51
Chapter Ten: Pushed by Two Angels	55
Chapter Eleven: The Preacher Who Beats His Innocent Dog	59
Chapter Twelve: Bread in the Briefcase	63
Chapter Thirteen: The Fifth Miracle at the Last Door	67
Chapter Fourteen: A Miracle at the Door	69
Chapter Fifteen: Another Miracle at the Door	71
Chapter Sixteen: Are You Going to Break Down My Door, Sir?	73
Chapter Seventeen: Yet Another Miracle at the Door	77

Chapter Eighteen: In Plain Sight but Not Seen	83
Chapter Nineteen: The Sixth Miracle at the Last Door	85
Chapter Twenty: The Book That Turned a Church 180 Degrees	91
Chapter Twenty-One: The Fourth Miracle at the Door	93
Chapter Twenty-Two: Saved from Suicide by Free at Last	99
Chapter Twenty-Three: FAQ at the Door	101
Chapter Twenty-Four: The Fifth Miracle at the Door	109
Chapter Twenty-Five: The Sixth Miracle at the Door	119
Chapter Twenty-Six: The Seventh Miracle at the Last Door	133
Chapter Twenty-Seven: The Last Miracle at the Last Door	135
Chapter Twenty-Eight: A Door of Opportunity for Everyone to Share the Gospel	139
Chapter Twenty-Nine: Practical Ways That My Family and I Share Our Faith	143
Chapter Thirty: Noah's Ark Was the Only Door of Hope	151
Conclusion	159
Bibliography	161

ACKNOWLEDGMENTS

Much thanks to my cousin, Leroy Jackson, for his excellent art work.

Special thanks to all who had been praying for me regarding this book project.

To Dave Spence, my faithful week day prayer partner. To Allan & Miriam Gayle for their prayers. To Dr. Daphne McNish, for her encouragement; Leroy Mohalland, my Wednesday morning prayer partner; and also to the numerous others who have prayed for me, in general. Your prayers have been heard, and the Lord had answered. To God be the glory.

Introduction

It was on a Friday night in January that the silence was broken by three knocks on the wooden side of the house, followed by the first cry that I uttered when I came into the world. It happened in that little house on the hillside in the Chovey district of Portland, Jamaica.

As I grew older, I was mostly in the loving care of my father and Malvina Richards, my god-fairing grand aunt. She was a very strict, sincere, and loving Christian woman. She loved me dearly and took great care in inculcating good manners and Christian values in me. She took me to church service every Sunday where my spiritual foundation was formally laid.

My environment was very peaceful, and people were kind, respectful, and looked out for each other. The scenery was quite rustic, and surrounding most of the homes in Chovey and the neighboring district of Chepstowe were cultivations of luxuriant gardens. Among the natural produce were yellow yam, coconuts, breadfruit, sugar cane, etc. Adding to all that beauty, was the tantalizing aromas filling the air from the diffusion of mangoes, jackfruits, oranges, soursop, star apples, and an array of many other exotic and succulent Jamaican fruits.

After a playful day of climbing mango trees, shooting birds, and frolicking in the sun with my friends, nightfall would lull me to sleep by the lullabies from the cacophony of crickets, toads, and croaking lizards, only to be awakened in the morning by the rooster's crow and the delightful dawn chorus of nightingales and mourning doves. It was very calming to listen to their echoing chirps augmented by the rushing waters of the Spanish River, as it reverberated from the surrounding hills that loomed in the distance.

By the time I was 8 years old, my father and mother both immigrated abroad, and I was left in the loving care of Aunt Malvina.

During those early years, I attended the primary school in the district of Skibo until 1966. That was the same year my aunt became ill and was admitted to the hospital. As a result, I relocated to the district of Kildare where I spent some time with my aunt, Estella Cross, and later moved to the town of Buff Bay, where I resided with Frank Solomon, my uncle. After Aunt Malvina passed, I spent the next four years with my uncle.

He was a great inspiration to me. I admired his ability to speak with ease and facility, and his amazing ability to seize attention with his command of the English language. To me, he was a paragon of eloquence. Apart from that, he had an enormous memory and was a repository in world history and politics. I gained tremendous admiration for my uncle, and I always wanted to emulate him.

How did he acquire such a wealth of knowledge? I came to the conclusion that he gained it not only because of his educational background but also because of his enormous reading habit. To my recollection, I hardly ever saw uncle Frank without a book in his hand 95 percent of the time.

Living with him allowed me to recognize how far behind I was in my own reading skills. At the age of thirteen, my reading and spelling skills were atrocious. Even though I had an excellent memory and could recite long poems taught to me by my aunt, I struggled to read the simplest of books. For some reason, I did not develop an early start in reading.

At the age of sixteen, I struggled to write a simple letter to a very lovely girl who showed an interest in me. I had to ask a good friend, Colin, to help me write that letter. My reading ability was below a fifth-grade level, and I struggled with it for years. As a result, it affected my life and educational path unto my mid-twenties.

During my teen years, I attended the Buff Bay Seventh-day Adventist Academy, and two years later, I was baptized as a member of the Seventh-day Adventist (SDA) Church. While attending the church, I became acquainted with a brother who was a colporteur (literature evangelist). I grew very curious about his work but never understood the true nature of it until ten years later.

In June of 1970, I immigrated to the United States where I reunited with my loving mother and my other siblings in the city of Philadelphia, Pennsylvania.

After graduating from West Philadelphia High School in 1972, my lack of focus and worldly allurements steered me into a world of fantasy. For a few years, my life was without direction and purpose like a ship on the ocean without a compass. Thankfully, like the prodigal son, who had wasted his time and fortune, the benevolent hands of God's amazing grace pulled me away from a precipice of self-destruction and back on to the Christian path.

Amazingly, my perspective on life began to change and took on a whole new purpose. Like a miracle, my reading ability soared immensely to an alarming level. The Bible, dictionaries motivational books, speeches, and seminars became my intimate friends, and I spent much quality time interacting with them. Intuitively, I realized that these were the things that would motivate

> *Thankfully, like the prodigal son, who had wasted his time and fortune, the benevolent hands of God's amazing grace pulled me away from a precipice of self-destruction and back onto the Christian path.*

and spur me onward with purpose and resoluteness. I knew this would eventually help to extricate me from the clutches of self-defeat and to greater enhancement in my life.

This revelation may seem alarming to many who know me. Some may even say, "That is not the Devon I know!" But in reality, those were the obstacles that I had to overcome in my life in order to reach the place where I am today.

I always carry with me the good counsels of my two favorite Pauls. Firstly, my former pastor, the late Paul Cantrell, who always greeted me by his famous line, "I hope that you will have the vision to see, the will to do, and the discipline to make it happen." And secondly, the apostle Paul who says, "I can do all things through Christ which strengtheneth me" (Phil. 4:13).

In 1976, while attending a Wednesday night prayer meeting service at the North Philadelphia Seventh-day Adventist Church, I heard a heartwarming testimony from Brother Lacey White, a literature evangelist. He spoke with great enthusiasm as he shared the wonderful experiences of God's blessing while working and selling his Christian literature.

I was deeply moved by his inspiring testimony and after the prayer meeting service, I asked him what it would take for me to get involved in that line of work. That Wednesday night became the turning point in my life on the journey of becoming a soul winner for Christ through the medium of literature evangelism.

In 1979, through God's providential working, I met and fell in love with Cynthia, a wonderful and adorable God-fearing young woman. Four years later in November of 1983, we were joined together as husband and wife. Together, we established a wonderful Christian home with a heavenly atmosphere and God blessed our union with two precious children, Khalilah and Daniel.

Working as a literature evangelist has been the most rewarding work that I have ever done in my life. I am very proud to have been and still be a member of this faithful army of Christian soldiers, who carry tidings of good news from country to country, city to city, street to street, and door to door, sharing the love of Jesus Christ in every corner of planet earth.

While most of my colleagues worked as full-time literature evangelists for the Family Health Education Service of the Allegheny East Conference of Seventh-day Adventists' publishing department, I, on the other hand, worked as a full-time employee at a medical institution. At the same time, I worked as a part-time literature evangelist. I am now retired from my regular employment, but I will never retire from the literature ministry as long as God allows me breath and strength to do so.

I am absolutely delighted to share within this book some of the most fascinating, soul-winning stories as well as some amazing encounters with danger. I will also share a few accounts of some of my faithful comrades. In addition, I will share how my wife and I endured our fiercest crucibles when adversity knocked at our own door and almost took the lives of our two wonderful children.

Whether you are Catholic, Jewish, Christian, Muslim, non-believer, or an atheist, this book will inspire you to share something from it to your friends and family.

So, then my friends, are you ready to whet your spiritual appetite? If you are, I invite you to join me on an incredible soul-winning journey. As we travel together from door to door, I promise that you will experience some of the most shocking and compelling twists and turns in Christian evangelism. It is my sincere hope that through this journey, your life experience will be marvelously enriched.

Sincerely, Devon L. Roberts

Chapter One

The First Rainy-Day Miracle at the Last Door

Just imagine a farmer praying desperately for some badly needed rain, while just across town others are setting up for a festive outdoor wedding ceremony and praying for bright and sunny day. Not to mention the season's opener baseball game getting ready to be started in town. Sunny day or rainy day? Whose prayer will be answered? Someone will have to set a rain date.

For the literature evangelists, however, setting a rain date is never an option. Come rain or shine, their work goes on in spite of weather challenges. Why are they so motivated? Is it due to the potential of making a profit? Not at all. It is because the object of their work is not mainly focused on temporal gains but rather on the winning of souls for Christ. That is the main reason for their amazing success.

> " For the literature evangelists, however, setting a rain date is never an option. Come rain or shine, their work goes on. "

From my personal experience, rainy days have been some of my most successful and rewarding days. Some of the following stories that I am about to share will reveal to you the reasons why.

Rainy-Day Miracles

Back in the early 1970s, when I first began to work as a literature evangelist, someone introduced me to a little book entitled, *The Greatest Salesman in the World.* In the book the author shares some wonderful secrets to success. One of those secrets that have been of great help to me is contained in just thirteen simple words which I memorized and have never forgotten: "Failure will never overtake you if your determination to succeed is strong enough" (Mandino, *The Greatest Salesman in the World*, p. 26). I did not comprehend the great significance and meaning of those powerful words until what I experienced in this first amazing success story.

A Freshman Salesman

One warm summer day in the city of Philadelphia, I decided to canvas on Chancellor Street where my Aunt Roseann lived. As the day passed on without my expected success, I began to get weary and discouraged, but what happened at the last door was beyond my wildest dream.

Here is how that day actually began. It was early afternoon when I first started knocking on doors on that little street of approximately sixty homes. From the early weather forecast, I knew that there would be rainy showers near the latter part of the evening, so I started early so that I could knock on as many doors as I possibly could ahead of the rain. With confidence and enthusiasm, I knocked on every single door on the left side of the street, but after hours of futile knocking, success eluded me. However, before venturing over to the other side, I decided to pause and pray with the hope of a greener pasture.

> As the day passed on without my expected success, I began to get weary and discouraged, but what happened at the last door was beyond my wildest dream.

Unfortunately, the situation grew even worse on the right side of the street. It was getting late, the sky was noticeably darker, and a slight drizzle could be felt every now and then. At that point, weariness began to slow me down and discouragement was trying to persuade me to quit. What should I do? I had knocked on 99 percent of the doors without a smidgen of success. I came to the conclusion that the best thing for me to do was go home all wet, haggard, and defeated.

From my natural human instinct, negative thoughts began to emerge. Why would the last door make a difference? And who would let a stranger into their home at that time of the evening? I realized that my faith was being tested, so, once again, I stood for a moment and prayed to God for His divine intervention in not allowing me to go home without a positive outcome.

With renewed courage and resoluteness, I knocked on that last door. At the first knock, there was no response, so I knocked again. Surprisingly, a lady, Mrs. Toffee, came to the door, peaked through the blinds, and asked who it was.

> *Why would the last door make a difference? And who would let a stranger into their home at that time of the evening?*

"My name is Mr. Roberts," I replied. "I am with the Family Health Education Service, and I am here in your community today sharing valuable information on health and well-being. You wouldn't mind if I stepped in for a few minutes while I explain, would you?" She apologized and said they were having dinner at the moment and asked that I come back another time. I found myself wondering what I should do. Should I just walk away and leave after I had just prayed for success or should I resort to what I had learned about how to handle objections? I decided to test the skills that I had learned and see how God would work it out.

Politely, I responded to Mrs. Toffee, "Mrs., I am so glad that you mentioned that, and since it is getting ready to rain, I'll be as brief as possible."

Hearing the conversation, her husband, Mr. Toffee, became concerned and inquired who it was that she was conversing with at the door. She told him that it was some man selling something. His response was quick. "Why don't you let him come in?" Those words sounded like music to my ears, and I stepped in with confidence and optimism.

Once I entered the house, Mr. Toffee greeted me and invited me to take a seat and relax until dinner was finished. Sitting at the dinner table with him was his wife and young children. As I sat there in the living room, I silently thanked God for allowing me entrance to the home and then prayed for a much-needed blessing.

The Largest Sale That I Had Ever Made

When dinner was finished and the table was cleared, they invited me to join the family at the table. As I began to give my presentation, highlighting some of the beautiful features of the children's Bible story books, he and his wife agreed that they wanted to purchase them for their children. Surprisingly, they asked me to show them all of the other books that I had. So, I showed them the bedtime story books, the medical set, the Bible reference library, and the list went on. Finally, they asked me to give them the total cost for all the books that I showed them. It was unbelievable; it amounted to hundreds of dollars. After we made a payment plan, they paid a sizable down payment.

That sale turned out to be one of the largest that I had ever made in one single home during the course of my literature work. What a mighty God we serve! Amidst disappointment, despondency, and rain, my day ended with an unimaginable success. The blessings gained from knocking on that one last door overshadowed all the negative elements that preceded it and made up for all the unanswered doors on Chancellor Street.

> "Amidst disappointment, despondency, and rain, my day ended with an unimaginable success. The blessings gained from knocking on that one last door over shadowed all the negative elements that preceded it and made up for all the unanswered doors."

In retrospect, the excerpt from *The Greatest Salesman in the World* made perfect sense. "Failure will never overtake you if your determination to succeed is strong enough."

Whenever Mrs. Toffee saw me after that, she would always challenge me by reminding me that she bought every book that I had. She would then ask if I had anything new and would purchase something for herself or for a friend. She was a continual customer for years.

"For the LORD God is a sun and shield: the LORD will give grace and glory: no good thing will he withhold from them that walk uprightly" (Ps. 84:11).

I am so glad that I did not yield to the tempter's sway but followed the direction of that still small voice. "I can do all things through Christ which strengtheneth me" (Phil. 4:13). The lesson that I learned from the Chancellor Street experience was to never give in and never give up, for God can work a miracle even at the last door.

Chapter Two

The Second Rainy-Day Miracle at the Last Door

They Believed and Were Baptized

I should have listened to the weather before I went out, but for some reason, I didn't. It was a Sunday morning in the winter of 1980, and I went out in the neighborhood placing postage-paid flyers advertising books and Bibles. In the process I ended up on South Cecil Street, not far from my home.

When I was just about to complete my mission, it suddenly started to rain very heavily. I didn't know it then, but I was actually standing on the porch of Ms. Patrina James' home when it started to rain, so I inserted the flyer in her door slot and made it my final door for the morning.

A couple of weeks later, I received a response card from one Patrina James requesting information about a nice, heirloom quality Bible that was available to purchase. Interestingly, that card was the only response that I received from the effort I had put forth on that rainy Sunday morning. Truthfully, that sole response card made me feel that my effort was not in vain.

Following Up

On February 19, 1980, I followed-up on the response card by making a visit to meet with Ms. James for the first time. After I introduced myself and the purpose of the call, she politely invited me into her home. She was a very calm and pleasant lady and so were her three delightful daughters as well as her mother and stepfather.

We sat around the dining table where it was convenient for everyone to see my presentation of the Heritage Bible. After showing them all the features of the Bible, Patrina liked it and made a down payment on it.

Unexpected Questions

Before I left the house that evening, Patrina began to ask me various questions concerning things in the Bible. I was very happy to see her interest, and I answered all of the questions that were asked to her satisfaction. The others were also quite impressed at the answers I gave, and as a result, each time when I would return to collect payment for the Bible, they would have more and more questions ready for me. They showed such insatiable desire in learning more about God's Word that it really touched my heart. Not only were they warm and friendly, but they made me feel very welcomed in their home. The Holy Scriptures tells us thusly: "But sanctify the Lord God in your hearts: and be ready always to give an answer to every man that asketh you a reason of the hope that is in you with meekness and fear" (1 Peter 3:15).

Sadly, just when I thought that I was getting to know the family, the time came when the Bible was paid off. I felt a deep sense of disappointment because I would not be seeing them any longer.

Thankfully, before leaving their home that final evening, I was impressed to offer them a free Bible study correspondence course. Amazingly, they were delighted at the suggestion, so Patrina along with her three daughters and her mother decided to enroll in the course. In a relatively short time, they all completed those lessons and were invited to visit my church on a special Sabbath to receive their certificate of completion.

Though they had finished the correspondence Bible lessons, I had a deep sense that they were still yearning to learn more about God's Word. With that impression, I asked them if they would be interested in an advanced Bible study course, which would be conducted right there in the convenience of their home. Without hesitation, they gladly agreed. When I explained to them that I would be personally conducting the study with them, they became even more delighted, so we made an arrangement for the study to be given on Friday evenings.

The Bible Studies

On that first Friday evening, I found the family waiting in eagerness, ready and well-prepared with their Bibles and notebooks.

During the course of the Bible studies, they told their friends and relatives about the new and exciting things that they were learning about the Bible and gladly invited them to come and sit in on the study. In fact, I even had the privilege of meeting their pastor, who was invited to come and sit in on the study. We had a wonderful time, and I got to know him well. When he learned that I was a part of a singing group, he invited my group to sing at his church.

As the Bible studies progressed, one of Patrina's nephews was also invited to join. He asked many questions and was amazed that the answers were all there in the Bible. He was deeply impressed with the studies, and in order not to miss out on any of them, he would come for the study on Friday nights and then stay over with the family until the next day.

There was also another young man named Jerry, who had close ties with the family, and he found the Bible studies to be quite interesting and would sit in from time to time. He was a very pleasant, friendly, and gregarious person. His cheerful and ebullient spirit always made us very happy when he attended the Bible study.

During one of the study sessions, Jerry told us that he had made a visit to his sister's church. While he was there, the minister, who purported to be a prophet, revealed a personal secret that stunned him. Jerry explained that the minister said that Jerry's vibration revealed that he was attending a Bible study along with some other people. It also revealed that the study was being conducted by a young man and that he should continue attending the study.

Jerry was puzzled as to how the minister would know all that personal information about him. "I was very confident that I had not told anyone that I was attending Bible studies," Jerry said.

The revelation that Jerry received from that clairvoyant minister did not sit well with him. Rather than having a positive effect, it made him very uncomfortable and apprehensive. As a result, Jerry never felt good about going back to visit that church.

So, the big question was, how did the minister know about Jerry's private activities? Was he a true prophet? We are not to judge people. Our duty is to study God's word for ourselves, live clean, pure, Godly lives, and leave the judgment of others to God. We should allow the Word of God to be our guide in every aspect of our lives. We should strive to be like Christ in every situation. When confronted with temptation and challenges, Jesus always resorted to, "It is written…" (Matt. 4:4).

Jerry's question was subsequently answered from the Word of God, as we delved deeper into the following Bible study topics: the gifts of the

Holy Spirit, the work of good and evil angels, the state of the dead, and spiritualism. The Holy Scriptures strongly admonish that in the last days there will be an increase of deceptive communication from the devil and his fallen angels. It happened to Adam and Eve in the Garden of Eden. They were a sinless couple made in the image of God, and their only safeguard against sin and deception was their obedience and reliance on God's word. If they were not exempted from temptation back then, none of us are exempted today.

You Will Know Them by Their Fruit

Before he found Jesus and became a Christian, Roger Morneau was deeply involved in devil worship. In his book, *Beware of Angels: Deceptions in the Last Days*, he gave these poignant words of caution:

> Let me add a few words of caution. Have nothing to do with hypnotists, fortunetellers, astrologers, palm readers, and psychics of any kind. Do not associate yourself in any way with professed Christians who converse with demonic spirits when they are 'driven out,' as in 'deliverance ministries.' And last, do not affiliate yourself with people who claim to talk with spirits of the dead. Such people are channels that evil spirits use to break through God's protection around people. (*Beware of Angels: Deceptions in the Last Days*, p. 47)

Jesus warns, "For there shall arise false Christs, and false prophets, and shall shew great signs and wonders; insomuch that, if it were possible, they shall deceive the very elect" (Matt. 24:24). Timothy also warns us this way, "Now the Spirit speaketh expressly, that in the latter times some shall depart from the faith, giving heed to seducing spirits, and doctrines of devils" (1 Tim. 4:1). The apostle John tells us plainly, "For they are the spirits of devils, working miracles, which go forth unto the kings of the earth and of the whole world, to gather them to the battle of that great day of God Almighty" (Rev. 16:14).

So, how can we positively know how to differentiate the true source of the communication?

The prophet Isaiah breaks it down this way:

> And when they shall say unto you, Seek unto them that have familiar spirits, and unto wizards that peep, and that mutter: should not a people seek unto their God? for the living to the dead? To the law and to

the testimony: if they speak not according to this word, it is because there is no light in them. (Isa. 8:19, 20)

Jesus, Himself, hit the nail on the head by saying, "Ye shall know them by their fruits. Do men gather grapes of thorns, or figs of thistles?" (Matt. 7:16).

God Added to the Church

At the conclusion of the Bible study, something great and exciting happened. Patrina, her three daughters, and her nephew decided that they wanted to be baptized.

It was a wonderful sight to witness, as all four of them, one by one, went down in the watery grave of baptism. It was a day of great rejoicing, as God added them as brand-new members to His church, but the story didn't stop there.

> *It was a wonderful sight to witness, as all four of them, one by one, went down in the watery grave of baptism. It was a day of great rejoicing, as God added them as brand-new members to His church, but the story didn't stop there.*

More Baptisms!

Shortly after their baptisms, Gianna Stelman, a very close friend, became interested and wanted to learn about Patrina's newfound faith, so she and her family visited the church one Sabbath to see what it was like. They had a wonderful worship experience. Gianna was moved in such a way that after the service she expressed a sincere desire to take Bible studies. Arrangements were made, and Bible studies were conducted by two faithful members from the church.

After some time, all heaven rejoiced as Gianna and three of her children took their stand and were also baptized into Christ. "Praising God, and having favour with all the people. And the Lord added to the church daily such as should be saved" (Acts 2:47).

Still, the story continued.

The Far-Reaching Effects of Our Christian Influences

On the week of April 24–30, 2022, the women's ministry department held some nightly meetings. During one of the nights, a medical doctor gave an excellent presentation on the importance of physical health to a woman's self-worth. She was the daughter of the women's ministry leader's brother.

In retrospect, it was forty plus years ago when I first knocked on Patrina's door. One of her daughters who was baptized after the Bible studies met the brother of our current women's ministry's leader at the church; he later became her husband. As a result of their union, they were blessed with two wonderful children. Today, they are still very happily married and are enjoying the successful accomplishments of their two children reared up through Christian education. One is an attorney, and the other is a medical doctor, the same one who spoke for this women's ministry event.

We may never know the far-reaching effect of our missionary endeavors until Jesus returns. Let us be encouraged to spread the love of Christ no matter what. Even if you are rejected, go to the next person and keep on sharing it in love. "I have planted, Apollos watered; but God gave the increase" (1 Cor. 3:6).

Chapter Three

The Third Rainy-day Miracle at the Last Door

Mission Accomplished

"God sent you here today, my son." Those were the words of Mrs. Munroe after I knocked on her door on a rainy Sunday morning in the fall of 1977.

In September of 1977, members of the Southwest Philadelphia Adventist Church were organized in various groups to go knocking on doors in a fundraising campaign. The objective was to collect monetary donations for disaster relief around the world.

My group decided to work the area in proximity of my home. While we were out there filling up our cans with donations, it suddenly began to rain, which put a damper on our mission. As a result, most of the people called it a day. In spite of the rain, I felt impressed and motivated to continue and knocked on a few more doors.

I ended up at 5913 Walnut Street as my final door. Why I decided to make that my final stop, I didn't know, but I followed through with my decision to complete my mission.

When I knocked on the door, a cheerful young woman, Jackie, looked out to see who it was and called to her mother. In a moment, Mrs. Munroe, a very friendly lady with a resplendent smile and a noticeable Jamaican accent, opened the door and asked who I was. Surprisingly, after a brief introduction, she invited me to step inside. I explained to her that I was with the community service of the Southwest SDA Church, and I was out collecting donations to help in disaster relief work around the world. I handed her a leaflet that highlighted what the donated funds were used for, and she happily gave a big donation.

What happened next was as an unexpected surprise.

Tears of Joy

Suddenly, Mrs. Munroe looked at me and broke down in tears and told me how happy she was that I had knocked on her door. She was convinced that God had sent me to her house. She explained that she was a faithful Seventh-day Adventist back in her country, but since she immigrated to the United States in 1968, she had not gone to church for all those years. Before she met me, she had been praying about going back to church, so she could start serving the Lord again, but for some unknown reason, she kept on procrastinating. However, that Sunday when I knocked on her door, she immediately knew that it was God's answer to her prayers.

After a few words of encouragement, I prayed with her and arranged to start Bible studies with the whole family on Friday evenings to get them back in the rhythm of things. When I left their home that Sunday afternoon, they were all excited and happy with eager anticipation.

> However, that Sunday when I knocked on her door, she immediately knew that it was God's answer to her prayers.

On that first Friday night when I arrived at the Munroe's home for Bible study, everyone was sitting down in readiness to sing hymns and have Friday evening worship. It was truly wonderful to see the joy that was rekindled in that home. It was a great Bible study session.

After a number of weeks, I spoke to Roberta, who was the Bible worker at my church, and told her about this new family with whom I had been studying. I asked her if it was possible for her to take over the Bible study, and she gladly consented. It wasn't long before eight members of the family started to attend church regularly every Sabbath. Finally, at the end of that study, they decided to recommit their lives to God and requested baptism.

On a beautiful Sabbath in the spring of 1978, Mrs. Munroe, her aged mother, and four of her daughters were baptized. Little did I know that was just the beginning.

More Baptisms

Subsequent to Mrs. Munroe's baptism, her husband, Wellesley, and two more daughters were baptized. Following that, her good friend, Princess, along with her daughter, Barbara, and son, Lenox, were baptized as well.

In addition, another of her friends, Mrs. Brown, and her husband, followed by their son, his wife, and later her niece were baptized. The ripple effect continued with multiple more baptisms of nieces, grand-nieces, and grandchildren, etc. As I write this book in the summer of 2022, forty-three souls and counting have been baptized as a result of knocking on Mrs. Munroe's door.

"And how shall they preach, except they be sent? as it is written, How beautiful are the feet of them that preach the gospel of peace, and bring glad tidings of good things!" (Rom. 10:15).

I did not realize it at the time, but in retrospect I could see the Lord's providential hands that guided me to continue knocking until the last door on that rainy Sunday morning. It was truly a miracle at the door, but that story did not end there.

> " I did not realize it at the time, but in retrospect I could see the Lord's providential hands that guided me to continue knocking until the last door on that rainy Sunday morning. "

How He Found His Wife

On Monday, May 23, 2022, a good friend and church brother, Earnie Davidson, came to look at my wife's car to ascertain whether she might need some new brakes. During our conversation, we talked about the good old days when we used to play basketball early on Sunday mornings back in the 1980s.

When he was about to leave, I handed him a few books in plastic bags designed to hang on door knobs, which he could use during his missionary endeavors. We spoke briefly of the far-reaching effect of the book ministry and the blessings of reaching people at their door. To illustrate my point, I told him what happened back in 1977, when I met the Munroe family on a rainy Sunday morning.

He laughed with great excitement when I pointed out to him that his wonderful wife, Annmarie, was among those grandnieces who were baptized in the Munroe family. Now he is enjoying his family, including four wonderful daughters and four grandchildren, as a result of one knock on the door of 5913 Walnut Street forty-five years ago on that rainy Sunday morning. He concurred by exclaiming, "To God be the glory! Great things He hath done!"

Chapter Four

The Fourth Miracle at the Last Door

Brighten the Corner Where You Live

When I walked through the door to give my condolences to Virginia, I didn't envision that this one Christian act in showing sympathy to others would result in the transformation of her daughter's life.

One of the first places that I started to knock on doors was the area surrounding my home. Often times, it seems that the people who are closest to us are sometimes the ones we find most difficult to work with or support, and they are generally more hesitant to appreciate the value of the work we do.

But every now and then, someone as close as our next-door neighbor brings us joy and encouragement. It is not strange that Jesus Christ Himself encountered the same problem with His own people and community in His day. Here is what the Scripture says: "But Jesus, said unto them, A prophet is not without honour, but in his own country, and among his own kin, and in his own house" (Mark 6:4).

So then, why should we count it strange when we find ourselves in a similar situation?

Back in the late seventies, I knocked on the door of my neighbor who lived in an apartment two doors down from me. The man of the house had suddenly died, so I wanted to express my condolences to Ms. Virginia. In the process, I met her daughter, Josephine, who had recently moved in with her since her recent loss.

In the course of my conversation with Josephine, the subject of church and Christianity came up, and before I left their apartment, I extended an invitation for to her to visit my church, and she graciously accepted the invitation. However, when I informed her that my worship service was held on Saturdays instead of Sundays, she was very surprised. I thought she might change her mind, but surprisingly, she kept her promise.

That Sabbath when Josephine visited my church, she was very impressed with the early Sabbath school program and orderly manner in which the worship service was conducted. But most of all, through the warm hospitality and friendliness of the members, she saw the love of Christ, and it made her feel right at home. That first Sabbath worship experience made a lasting impression on Josephine's mind and played a major part of her later decision.

One Sunday morning, I decided to reciprocate by paying a surprise visit to her church, the 59th Street Baptist church. She was not expecting to see me, so it resulted in a very happy and unexpected surprise.

Bible Study

Josephine was a very humble, sincere, and dedicated Christian young woman who genuinely loved the Lord. When I offered to study the Bible with her, she did not hesitate; she gladly accepted the opportunity to learn more about God's Word. Being a sincere Christian, she believed in the plan of salvation through the love and sacrifice of Jesus Christ; however, she had a longing to learn more about Bible prophecies and other topics. Studying about the state of the dead was very reassuring, considering the recent loss of a loved one.

During the course of the Bible study, she would pay a visit to my church every now and then, but when she learned more about other truths, which she had not previously been exposed to, she became convinced through the Word of God that she needed to make changes in her life.

> *Little did I know that visit in showing sympathy to others would result as a wonderful miracle at the door.*

As the studies continued, Josephine became convicted on the wonderful new truths that she was learning. She couldn't hold back any longer, so she decided to take a positive step towards her newfound faith. She was baptized and became a very active member of the church.

I am very happy that when the Lord impressed me to brighten the corner where I lived, Josephine saw the light and gladly decided to walk in it. Little did I know that visit in showing sympathy to others would result as a wonderful miracle at the door.

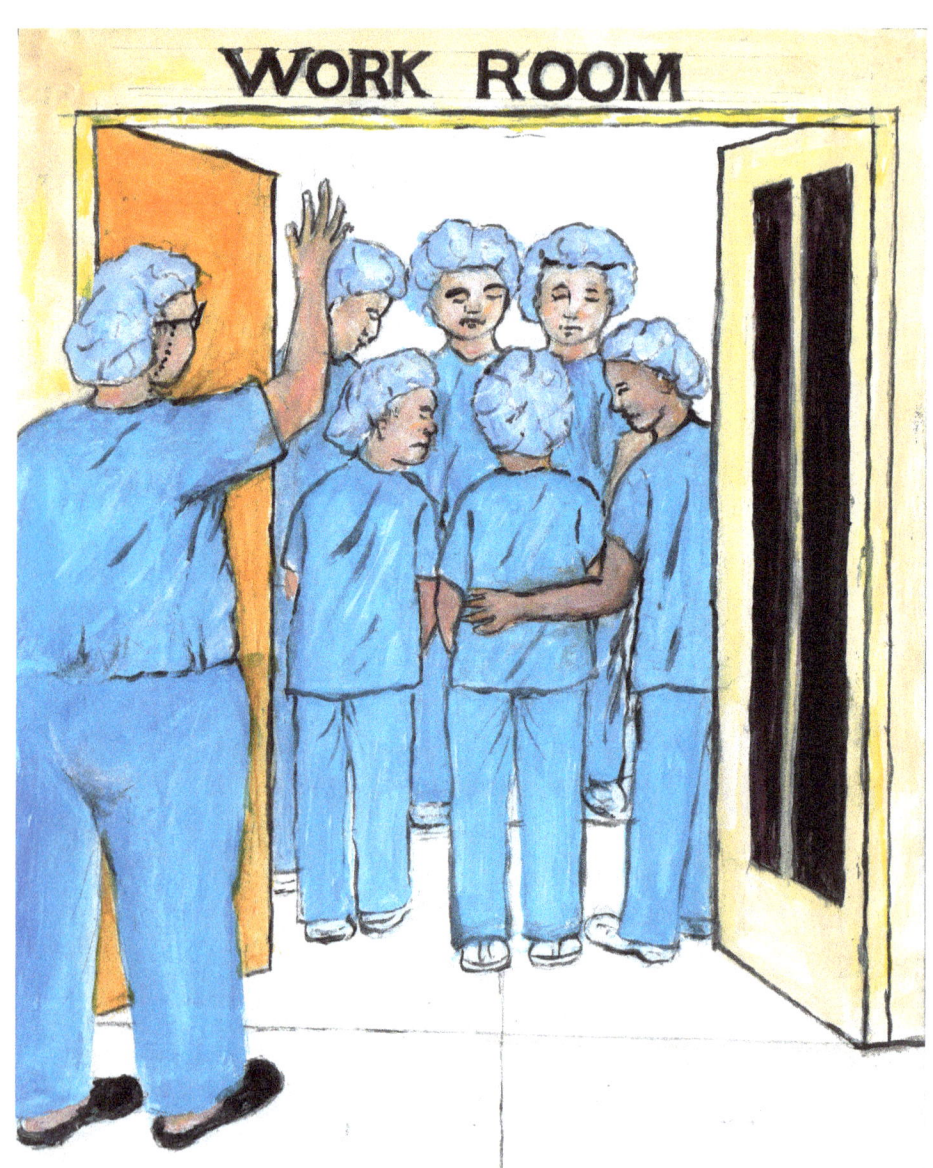

Chapter Five

A Miracle at My Work Room Door

Brighten the Corner Where You Work

"Why is this door closed? Find another place to do your prayers not in the operating room suite. Furthermore, this door should not be closed when I need access to it." Those were the firm words spoken to us by Dr. Sweden, as a few coworkers and I huddled together to pray in the anesthesia work room.

In 2007, I was transferred to a new location where Dr. Sweden was the medical director. While in this new environment, my co-workers came to notice my Christian conduct. Their assessments of my character were based on my overall demeanor and my thoughtfulness and consideration towards others. They also heard the soft soothing hymns and instrumental music that came from my work room. It was noted that whenever someone was frustrated or despondent, I would show concern by quietly asking if they would like me to pray for them.

Soon after their prayers were answered, they would tell others, and as the word got around the department, it inspired others to come to me with their prayer requests. It got to a place where some of my new co-workers earnestly requested me to pray with them every morning before they would start their workday. They truly believed that prayer would help set the tone for a peaceful working environment at the start of the day.

A Place to Pray

The space where I worked was called the anesthesia work room. It was a small room, which was approximately nine by fifteen feet, where necessary supplies for anesthesia are kept. This was the only private space that we found convenient enough to gather in the mornings to meet and have a brief word of prayer.

I was very impressed with the genuineness of the people in wanting to come together and pray to start off the day. The number of us grew until we could hardly fit into that crowded little space, but it felt great doing it and brought a sense of peace and tranquility.

One morning as me and my prayer pals were all gathered together for a brief prayer, Dr. Sweden knocked on the door. She urgently needed to collect some items from the work room. But because the door was briefly closed and was not immediately opened to her urgent nock, she became agitated and shouted, "What's going on in there? Why is this door closed?" When she saw us huddled to pray, she sternly said, "Find another place to do your prayers, not in the operating room suite. This door should not be closed when access is needed."

It was bad judgment on our part, and we knew that she was right to react the way she did. We would have reacted the same way if, on the other hand, we needed access to supplies that were urgently needed and could not have immediate access to it.

We honestly had not thought about it when we decided to use the work room for prayer, so everyone sincerely apologized.

Eventually, my work room became a center of influence and through the working out of God's providences, three special miracles happened where my Christian influence played a major part.

A Portentous Dream

About a month after the closed-door incident, I had a very strange dream about Dr. Sweden. In that dream I saw her sitting in her office and crying bitterly, while giving comfort to a young man who was resting on her shoulder as if he were her own son. The dream was so impressive that I felt impelled to talk to her about it. I prayed about it and gathered the courage to speak with her about the dream.

One morning shortly after, I asked her for a moment to speak with her privately in her office, and she agreed. As she sat at her desk, I stood, and in a very calm and earnest manner, explained to her what I had dreamed about. I told her that I did not know what it meant but that from time to time, God shows me things in dreams before they were actually manifested.

Before I left her office, I assured her that I had prayed about what I had dreamed, and she honestly thanked me for sharing it with her.

The Accident

Unfortunately, as I arrived at work about a month or so later, I heard the sad news that her son, her only child, had been in a terrible motor vehicle accident and was in critical condition in the intensive care unit hanging on to life. The doctors were fearful that he might die if he didn't have certain procedures done which were critical to his survival.

Earnest Prayers

The entire surgical center staff were deeply moved with heartfelt love, sympathy, and compassion, and we all earnestly prayed on behalf of Dr. Sweden for her son to pull through.

In the meantime, Dr. Sweden took a leave of absence from work to deal with her unexpected crisis. During that time, the Holy Spirit moved upon my heart to write her a sincere note of hope and encouragement to help assuage her pain while she was going through that rough and uncertain period.

Encouraging Words

When Dr. Sweden returned to work, she called me into her office and with tears in her eyes, she embraced me and expressed her loving gratitude for my prayers and thoughtfulness. She told me the card that she received from me meant a lot to her. It gave her hope, encouragement, and great solace, which she badly needed during those trying times.

All of us in the department were very happy at the remarkable outcome in the recovery of her son. We were truly convinced without a doubt that our united prayers of faith played a great part in his full recovery.

Even though we were not able to find another convenient location to pray, I have learned to not hold on to resentment against a person upon the basis of a temporary bout of displeasure. Everyone at some point in their lives has experienced some form of displeasure or anger against someone's action. We should never take it personally and carry around a chip on our shoulder. That person may have long forgotten the incident and moved on in their happy lives while we are still carrying that ponderous baggage of resentment.

Working with Dr. Sweden was a great delight. I found her to be a most tenderhearted, kind, and benevolent person. Her genuineness of character was demonstrated to me in the way she reciprocated her thoughts and sympathy when my father passed in 2011.

How marvelous it was to experience a living miracle right there through the influence of my work room door and how the power of united prayers can bring unexpected blessing when we administer to the needs of others.

However, that was not the end. There were yet two more miracles as a result of my work room experience.

Chapter Six

Another Miracle at My Work Room Door

A Coworker's Desperate Plea

On account of my spiritual influence around the work place, one of my coworkers, a very pleasant and excellent operating room tech, reached out to me with an urgent concern. She explained that there were some strange and mysterious things of a supernatural nature taking place in her home. She stated that, at times, family members would see an apparition in the kitchen, and at other times, the lights would go on and off and music would play without anyone turning it on. The occurrences were becoming more frequent, and the situation was getting very desperate, causing fear and anxiety among her family members.

In listening to her dilemma, I had no doubt of what was happening. For some reason, the power of darkness was manifesting its presence in a very bold and open manner in her home. Her question was if anything could be done to stop those mysterious activities. The first thing I did was to rule out the thought that the manifestation was not the spirit of the dead. In fact, contrary to a common belief, deceased people are not even aware of the fact that they themselves are deceased.

An Analogy

For example, she and I both worked in the operating room. Her work was more focused on the surgical while mine was on anesthesia. During our work we both had the opportunity to observe hundreds of patients go under anesthesia. To my understanding and observation, when patients are put to sleep under general anesthesia, they don't feel pain because they are completely unconscious and therefore oblivious to anything that transpires during surgery. Whether the procedure took one hour or ten hours, there is practically no memory of the passage of time between the moment they are put to sleep and the time they wake up.

Many times, when patients are coming out of anesthesia, it seems to them as though only a few seconds had transpired when, in fact, many hours may have passed during their surgery. Sometimes the patients may even ask upon waking, "When are they going to start the surgery?" This is because there is no consciousness of the passing of time while they were asleep.

The vast difference in contrast to a patient being under anesthesia is that anesthesia can be reversed and the unconscious person wakes up, but when a person dies, that very moment, time and consciousness cease to exist permanently.

To clarify this point, the wise man Solomon unequivocally states, "For the living know that they shall die: but the dead know not any thing, neither have they any more a reward; for the memory of them is forgotten" (Eccles. 9:5).

The psalmist David also affirms, "His breath goeth forth, he returneth to his earth; in that very day his thoughts perish" (Ps. 146:4).

"He shall return no more to his house, neither shall his place know him anymore" (Job 7:10).

So, with the analogy of an unconscious patient under anesthesia compared with a deceased person and the confirmation of the Scriptures, it is very clear that my coworker's house was not being haunted by the spirit of any unconscious deceased person, but rather from some other source outside the natural boundaries.

Hope Returns

I told my coworker about a similar situation where a young woman was having difficulty combatting such spiritual activity in her house as well. But thankfully, for her, after much prayer and fasting by a few faithful elders and prayer partners, God intervened and put an end to her nightmare.

My coworker became very hopeful when she heard the story and asked if I could help in her situation as well. I assured her that there was nothing too hard for God to do. Following my conversation with her, I consulted with a faithful elder of my church about the matter.

Because of the urgent nature of the situation, we immediately prepared ourselves by prayer and fasting and then arranged for a visit to her home the next Sabbath.

Accompanying me on that Sabbath visit was elder Leroy Mohalland and a couple sisters from the church, namely Joyce David and Matlhatso Reed. Before we entered to the home, we prayed earnestly for guidance and for the presence of the Holy Spirit.

When we arrived at the home, my coworker greeted us with gladness. I asked her to gather all the family members together, so we could offer a few uplifting words of encouragements.

The Power of Prayer and Faith

Elder Mohalland led out in prayer and earnestly poured out his heart to God, and through the mighty power of the name of Jesus, he asked for God's blessing upon the house. He prayed for the protection of the family members and for the permanent eviction of the demonic forces from the premises. He ended his prayer by asking for God's abiding presence to remain in the home through the blood of His Son, Jesus Christ.

Anointing the Lintel and the Two Side Posts

When he was finished praying, we anointed the lintel and the two side posts of the doors where one enters the house and kitchen with olive oil. Following that, a brief benediction was offered then we wished the family God's blessings.

Before we left the home, there was a feeling of peace and tranquility. My coworker expressed her gratitude and so did the rest of the family.

"And he called unto him the twelve, and began to send them forth by two and two; and gave them power over unclean spirits" (Mark 6:7).

"And they overcame him by the blood of the Lamb, and by the word of their testimony; and they loved not their lives unto the death" (Rev. 12:11).

Several times subsequent to that Sabbath visit to my coworker's home, I asked her if there were any recurrence of unusual activity around the home. It makes me glad to say that her answer was none at all. She and her family won our trust not because of what we did but what God was able to do through us. That was truly a miracle at the door through the tremendous power of the blood of Jesus Christ.

Chapter Seven

The Works of Fallen Angels Continue

One day a coworker asked me if it was wrong for her to visit a medium in order to obtain information about her future. These are valid questions that people ask, and I believe it is important to share what the biblical perspective is in regards to such questions.

The work of fallen angels is very prevalent all over the world today, and it has been that way among humankind ever since Adam and Eve, through curiosity, fell victims by that deception about 6,000 years ago.

In my small district of Chovey in Portland, Jamaica, I grew up accustomed to hearing many ghost stories. I remembered the lurid details of the White Witch of Rose Hall. I cannot express how fearful it was for me thinking of an encounter with the Rolling Calf, Ball of Fire, Jumbee Man, or the Duppy Woman. These spooky and ghostly legends were real in my mind as well as in the minds of those who I grew up around.

Witchcraft was and is still very prevalent today. Many people still go to an obeah man (voodoo doctor) to fix their so-called problems. Some go to try and work evil against others or to inquire whether their husbands or wives are cheating. Still, others go to find out who may be working evil on them and then try to return the favor. Such is the mindset and practice for many people around the world today. The mysterious works of fallen angels are not fake but very real. I have experienced it and have witnessed it with my very own eyes.

> "
> *The mysterious works of fallen angels are not fake but very real. I have experienced it and have witnessed it with my very own eyes.*
> "

When My Aunt Malvina Died

When I was thirteen years of age, my Aunt Malvina was getting old and sickly, so I became her hands and feet. As time went on, her illness got worse, and she was hospitalized in the little town of Buff Bay. I was living with my Uncle Frank, and while there, I was able to visit the hospital and see my aunt every day.

On a warm Tuesday evening in September of 1966 after leaving school, I went to see her in the hospital. "How are you, my darling?" was her weak but compassionate voice. "Come close to me, son." She gave me a hug as tears fell from her eyes. She asked me to fix her head in a comfortable position on her pillow which made her feel better. She said they were planning to take her to the university hospital in Kingston the next day. With sadness in her voice, she explained to me how sick she was feeling and that she didn't think that she would be around in this life much longer. Then with tears still running down her face, she said to me, "Devon, you must take care of yourself, son." I felt strange and saddened when she said those ominous words. And even though I was now living with caring relatives, the thought of being without her gave me the sense of loneliness, despondency, and a void that was not fillable.

Will Your Spirit Come Back to Hurt Me?

That was the fearful question that I asked my aunt after pondering what she had said about her not being around much longer.

I went close to her ears and earnestly asked, "Aunty, if you should you die, will your duppy (spirit) come back to hurt me?" She knew how I was feeling and her heart of compassion went out to me.

She called me close to her and softly said, "No, darling, I would never hurt you. I would protect you instead." With those reassuring words, my fears were assuaged. Then she reminded me that I should not come to visit her the next day since they would be taking her to the university hospital. As I said goodbye, she turned to watch me as I walked away, and I kept looking back at her all the way to the door. As I exited the hospital ward, I was overwhelmed with great sadness in my heart. Little did I know that it would be the last time I would see my loving Aunt Malvina alive in this life.

The following morning as I was getting ready for school, one of my older cousins, Sislyn, who lived in Buff Bay, came by to tell the sad news. Referring to my aunt, she said, "Devon, Mum is gone."

My response was, "I know; she told me that she would be going to the university hospital today." Sislyn figured out that I did not understand her euphemism, so she came close, put her hand on my shoulder, and tactfully said, "Mum died last night."

The impact of her passing did not affect me then at thirteen years of age. I did not shed a tear until later in my adult life when I really understood how dearly I loved and missed her.

Aunty, if you should die, will your duppy (spirit) come back to hurt me?

This question that I asked my aunt on her dying bed was motivated from my ignorance of the state of the dead. I was brought up to think that when a person dies, they really did not actually die. I thought that their mortal body was the only thing that perished, but their spirit left the body at death and either went to heaven to be with God forever or to a place called hell where they would be burned in everlasting fire. That is what I was led to believe, and I accepted it wholeheartedly until I later learned the truth by sincere Bible study.

Misled By A Song

As a young lad growing up on the island, I remembered a certain calypso song that was played on the radio every morning when getting ready for school. The essence of the song, as I recall, tells the story of a living person running from a ghost. The lyrics of the song explained the frightful experience of a brave young man who had decided take a walk through a cemetery during the night.

While walking through the darkness of the cemetery ground, his foot accidently got caught in the root of a mango tree, and he subsequently fell inside a tomb. A ghost spoke to him from the tomb and said not to be afraid and invited him instead to join him in playing a card game. Filled with absolute horror, the young man zoomed his way out of the tomb and fled with lightning speed towards the cemetery gate. As he reached the gate, he met a tall gentleman, and in his gasping breath, started to tell him about the frightful encounter. The tall man seemed quite solicitous and listened patiently, but then he gave a response.

He said how he understood what a brave and intrepid young man he was. According to the song, the next statement that the tall gentleman uttered created more horror to the young man and sent him running away perhaps even much faster than an Olympian. What was it that the tall gentleman said in response? "When I was alive," said the gentleman, "I used to do the same." Let's be honest, who wouldn't run at the utterance of such a creepy statement at that time of night? Now that I am much more enlightened from the Scriptures as to the state of the dead, my response would most likely be different.

There was a mysterious element of confusion in the song that didn't seem to fit into the heaven or hell narrative. But I still believed it just as many thousands of others do. Why did I hang on to such belief? It was because it came from the mouths of trusted parents, respected preachers, and notable celebrities, etc.

Now if departed loved ones were in heaven as I was taught, then seriously thinking, when would they have time to leave the bliss of the heavenly courts to return as a ghost to walk at nights and even protect their living relatives or meddle in earthly affairs? And for those unfortunate ones who wound end up in hell, would they not come back to warn their friends and relatives to live a godly life, so they wouldn't end up in such a horrible place?

Often times I think of the many innocent people who met their untimely death at the hand of vicious murderers leaving the lives of loved ones wrecked and empty.

I asked myself why in the world can't some of these dead people return from the dead or send messages to the district attorney's office as to who killed them? How could they be happy in heaven while their loved ones left on earth are going through suffering and grief, offering thousands of dollars in reward for someone to solve the mystery of their demise?

The answer to all these bothersome and perplexing questions began to unravel as I started to diligently study the Scriptures in search of the truth. As I began to peruse the Bible for the real truth about the state of the dead, I was released from many of my youthful fears that had prompted me to ask my aunt the question that I did.

Before I studied the Scriptures, I would not dare walk alone through a graveyard or pass by a gravesite in the dark of night like the young man in that song. My ignorance held me captive and my night time activities were circumscribed by unnecessary fears of ghosts and duppies.

Some of the things I am about to share may challenge some of the long-held beliefs of some people. Others may be motivated to study their Bible more diligently than ever before or question their pastors and priests about the state of their departed loved ones.

A Murderous Evil Spirit

It was quite early on Tuesday morning, September 4, 1984, when my wife and I were awakened from an ominous telephone call from one of her sisters. Apparently, my wife's mother, upon arriving home from an exhausting weekend trip to Canada, intended to return straight to work without adequate time off to rest. She suddenly fell ill and was taken by ambulance to the emergency room.

When we arrived at the emergency room, the sight and sound of lamentation made us suspect that the worst had happened. Sadly, she had suffered a massive heart attack and was not able to pull through. It was absolutely devastating for my wife and her six other siblings with the sudden loss of their dear, loving mother, Joyce, who was the glue that kept the whole family united.

A day or so later, one of my sisters-in-law boldly stated that her mother's spirit would rise on the third day. I became embroiled in the conversation and stated that the Scriptures did not support such a view. But she was adamant in her belief, so to prove my point, I decided that on the third night, I would sleep in her mom's room on her own bed since no one else was brave enough to do so. Finally, that night came, and I was faithful to my word and slept on my mother-in-law's bed alone in her room.

At about 2:30 a.m. that morning, I was suddenly awakened. I became aware that I was not alone in the room and that the atmosphere was not friendly. It seemed to me that the evil one was not happy with what I had done and was about to try and take my life if he could. I was fully conscious of what was transpiring but felt paralyzed. As I began to mentally assess the situation, I realized that I could hardly open my eyes, but when I was able to, I saw a dark form bending over me. I could not move or speak, but my heart was pounding heavily within my chest. Then as if to prove a point, the creature or being, or whatever it was, began to suppress my breathing by compressing my whole body like a blood pressure cuff around an arm. I wanted to scream and shake off whatever it was that was oppressing me, but I had no control and could not even as much as blink my eyes much less move. Fearful thoughts and

> *As if to prove a point, the creature or being, or whatever it was, began to suppress my breathing by compressing my whole body like a blood pressure cuff around an arm. I wanted to scream and shake off whatever it was that was oppressing me, but I had no control and could not even as much as blink my eyes much less move.*

questions began to saturate my mind. Would I remain in this condition to the point of death? I wondered if anyone else was nearby, but everyone else was asleep and was not aware of my dilemma.

With desperation, a thought of prayer flashed through my consciousness and the name of Jesus flooded my mind. I knew I had no power to speak, but with the power of my will and thought, I desperately called out the name of Jesus. Instantly, like the sudden gush of wind, the dark shadow made its flight and vanished through the closed window. Instantaneously, I regained all of my faculties and jumped out of bed. My heart filled with gratitude, and I poured out my thanks to God for His grace in delivering me from the oppressive power of the prince of darkness. When daylight came, I shared my encounter with the rest of the family.

> "With desperation, a thought of prayer flashed through my consciousness and the name of Jesus flooded my mind. I knew I had no power to speak, but with the power of my will and thought, I desperately called out the name of Jesus."

Who Was It?

According to Job, it is absolutely clear that it could not have been the spirit of my deceased mother-in-law because the Word of God very clearly and unequivocally refutes that idea: "As the cloud is consumed and vanisheth away: so he that goeth down to the grave shall come up no more. He shall return no more to his house, neither shall his place know him anymore" (Job 7:9, 10). Furthermore, the book of 2 Samuel amplifies it this way, "But now he is dead, wherefore should I fast? can I bring him back again? I shall go to him, but he shall not return to me" (2 Sam. 12:23).

Here are some more texts that point to this same conclusion:

"Beloved, believe not every spirit, but try the spirits whether they are of God: because many false prophets are gone out into the world" (1 John 4:1).

"Even him, whose coming is after the working of Satan with all power and signs and lying wonders, And with all deceivableness of unrighteousness in them that perish; because they received not the love of the truth, that they might be saved. And for this cause God shall send them strong delusion, that they should believe a lie" (2 Thess. 2:9–11).

"For we wrestle not against flesh and blood, but against principalities, against powers, against the rulers of the darkness of this world, against spiritual wickedness in high places" (Eph. 6:12).

Thanks be to God, we have a defense against these dark forces in Jesus. "Behold, I give unto you power to tread on serpents and scorpions, and over all the power of the enemy: and nothing shall by any means hurt you" (Luke 10:19).

"Jesus Christ the same yesterday, and to day, and for ever" (Heb. 13:8).

The only means by which a deceased person can ever come back to life in any form and in any way is by a resurrection. The same way Jesus was resurrected is the very same way we will be resurrected. Any other form of consciousness in death is not biblical. We must rely on Scripture and Scripture alone.

"The dead praise not the LORD, neither any that go down into silence" (Ps. 115:17).

"For the grave cannot praise thee, death can not celebrate thee: they that go down into the pit cannot hope for thy truth" (Isa. 38:18).

"If a man die, shall he live again? all the days of my appointed time will I wait, till my change come" (Job 14:14).

"Behold, I shew you a mystery; We shall not all sleep, but we shall all be changed, In a moment, in the twinkling of an eye, at the last trump: for the trumpet shall sound, and the dead shall be raised incorruptible, and we shall be changed." (1 Cor. 15:51, 52).

"For the Lord himself shall descend from heaven with a shout, with the voice of the archangel, and with the trump of God: and the dead in Christ shall rise first. Then we which are alive and remain shall be caught up together with them in the clouds, to meet the Lord in the air: and so shall we ever be with the Lord" (1 Thess. 4:16, 17).

Misunderstood Bible Verses

The Word of God was the source that unshackled me from the erroneous views that held me captive from my early teens. Sometimes I came across Bible verses that seemed to allude that people who die go directly to heaven at their death. But when these isolated verses are placed line upon line with the whole Bible in their context, the real truth emerges that there are only two ways to get to heaven. Firstly, by translation, like with Elijah and Enoch, who did not see death. Secondly, by resurrection, like with Moses and the multitudes who were resurrected on Easter Sunday morning along with Jesus. There is not a third option.

Job clearly states, "If a man die, shall he live again? all the days of my appointed time will I wait, till my change come" (Job 14:14). When will that appointed time be?

The apostle Paul states, "Henceforth there is laid up for me a crown of righteousness, which the Lord, the righteous judge, shall give me at that day: and not to me only, but unto all them also that love his appearing" (2 Tim. 4:8). When will the appearing be?

The apostle James also amplifies this point. "Blessed is the man that endureth temptation: for when he is tried, he shall receive the crown of life, which the Lord hath promised to them that love him" (James 1:12).

When will we receive our rewards? The apostle John explains. "And, behold, I come quickly; and my reward is with me, to give every man according as his work shall be" (Rev. 22:12). The obvious answer is when Jesus comes with His rewards.

> Let not your heart be troubled: ye believe in God, believe also in me. In my Father's house are many mansions: if it were not so, I would have told you. I go to prepare a place for you. And if I go and prepare a place for you, I will come again, and receive you unto myself; that where I am, there ye may be also. (John 14:1–3)

Jesus promised to come again to receive us to where He is not that we would join Him at our death. He is coming to get us. That's why Job said that he will wait. Furthermore, that is the reason that apostle Paul states,

> But I would not have you to be ignorant, brethren, concerning them which are asleep, that ye sorrow not, even as others which have no hope. For if we believe that Jesus died and rose again, even so them also which sleep in Jesus will God bring with him. For this we say unto you by the word of the Lord, that we which are alive and remain unto the coming of the Lord shall not prevent them which are asleep. For the Lord himself shall descend from heaven with a shout, with the voice of the archangel, and with the trump of God: and the dead in Christ shall rise first: Then we which are alive and remain shall be caught up together with them in the clouds, to meet the Lord in the air: and so shall we ever be with the Lord. Wherefore comfort one another with these words. (1 Thess. 4:13–18)

Chapter Eight

Another Remarkable Miracle at My Work Room Door

The miracles at my work room door did not stop at my coworker's plea for help from the supernatural encounter at her home. Another astonishing and unbelievable development was taking place that would end up being the acme of the entire work room episode.

Our imperceptible God was doing something fantastic behind the scenes of which I was totally oblivious. Jane, a coworker and friend, was an active participant in the prayer group. She was very impressed and sincerely moved by the spiritual atmosphere that was being generated from the little prayer group on the job. It caused a refreshing and transforming effect on her life. She even told me a number of times that God was speaking to her through me, which made us bond even more spiritually.

Thanks to Her Son

In conversing with Jane, she told me that she was raised in a family who were faithful, dedicated, and sincere Roman Catholics.

While her son, David, was in college, he joined a Bible study group, and after noting his excitement about the Bible, it aroused her interest, and she began studying as well. She fell in love with the Bible, and as she began learning more biblical truths, she followed her convictions. As a result, she found herself gravitating more and more towards what the Bible teaches while moving away from the traditional doctrines and teaching of the catechism. She was convicted through her own introspection and felt her need to know more about God and get closer to Him.

Noting her enthusiasm and insatiable desire to learn more about the Bible, I introduced her to the Amazing Facts correspondence Bible course, which she loved. Upon its completion, she continued in a personal one-to-one Bible study with Lillian, a Bible worker from the Chestnut Hill SDA Church.

Her Baptism

Then came the big day. On Sabbath, May 22, 2010, my family and I visited the Chestnut Hill Seventh-day Adventist Church to witness a very special miracle. It was very special because Jane was to be baptized as a born again, Bible-believing, commandment-keeping, Sabbath-observing Christian. It was truly remarkable to see. Standing by her side was her loving husband, daughter, and son, all there in a show of loving support and to witness a true miracle.

I am so glad that through God's benevolent mercies and infinite wisdom, He used my work room as a door of hope and opportunity for me to shine His light to brighten the corner where I work. Jane's baptism was truly a remarkable miracle at the door.

> *Through God's benevolent mercies and infinite wisdom, He used my work room as a door of hope and opportunity for me to shine His light to brighten the corner where I work.*

"And we know that all things work together for good to them that love God, to them who are the called according to his purpose" (Rom. 8:28).

Chapter Nine

Are You an Angel?

"Are you an angel?" That was the unexpected question that was posed to me by Onekha Melnor, as her eyes focused on the picture of an angel on the page of a book that I had just opened to her.

On April 16, 1998, a group of literature evangelists gathered at my home for a short meeting before going out to knock on doors in my neighborhood. One of the objectives of canvassing my area was to gather interest for Bible studies, which would eventually materialize into the establishment of a mission and, eventually, the establishment of a church in the area. After the meeting we all went out to various locations in proximity to my home.

On one of the first doors that I knocked on, I was greeted by a kind and friendly young lady with a welcoming smile and a winsome spirit.

As I introduced myself and opened one of the books, her face lit up in surprise when her eyes caught sight of the picture of an angel. "Wow! That is really strange," she said. "Just a short while ago before you came, I was in a conversation with someone talking about angels, and here you are at my door, showing me a book with the picture of an angel." Then, to my surprise, she looked at me strangely and asked, "Are you an angel?"

I was unprepared for that question, but I quickly assured her that I was not an angel but a servant of God. I confidently told her that it could be that God in His providence sent me with a special message just for her.

> "
> Just a short while ago before you came, I was in a conversation with someone talking about angels, and here you are at my door, showing me a book with the picture of an angel." Then, to my surprise, she looked at me strangely and asked, "Are you an angel?.
> "

I conveyed the thought to her that based upon the infallible Scriptures, angels were present as we talked together and that they also walk along with me as I go from door to door. She was very pleased with my answer and purchased the book. My prayer for her was that as she read the book along with the Bible, God would open her heart to a deeper understanding of His Word and help her develop a loving relationship with Jesus.

As I walked away from the door, I felt even more cognizant of the presence of the ministering angels.

"Are they not all ministering spirits, sent forth to minister for them who shall be heirs of salvation?" (Heb. 1:14).

"And he said unto me, The LORD, before whom I walk, will send his angel with thee, and prosper thy way..." (Gen. 24:40).

Guardian Angels

Personally, I have never seen my guardian angel, but I know indubitably that he is with me at all times. I call him Partner, and sometimes I speak to him, just to let him know that I am aware of his presence with me. Sometimes I am ashamed of the things I say and do, forgetting that he is there. I know that many times over the years I have made him sad and disappointed because of my unfaithfulness to God. However, I thank God for assigning him to me. That assurance keeps me ever conscious of his presence, his loving care, and guardianship over me.

One day real soon when Jesus returns, I am very sure that Partner, my celestial guardian and friend, will be the one to escort me to meet Jesus in the air. What a day of rejoicing that will be, when he formally introduces himself to me. I cannot imagine how I will react when he reveals his sympathetic loving care, his interests, and his countless interventions in ministering on behalf of my salvation during my earthly life. How will I express my gratitude?

"Bless the LORD, ye his angels, that excel in strength, that do his commandments, hearkening unto the voice of his word" (Ps. 103:20).

All praises to God, the Father, and to my loving Savior, Jesus Christ, for the loving ministry of angels!

Chapter Ten

Pushed by Two Angels

"Where did they go?" Mary exclaimed. *They certainly would have had to reverse their car to get out of my street!* Mary said to herself, as she stood there in absolute astonishment as her two helpers vanished out of sight.

When you talk about a hard-working person, Mary Flowers was one of such persons. She was an arduous worker in the field of literature evangelism, and to me, she was as a perfect example of who a true literature evangelist should be.

As an associate publishing director of the Allegheny East Conference of Seventh-day Adventists, Mary made sure that books were available to all who worked under her leadership. Often times, I would visit her home to collect books and vice versa. She would even deliver them to my home when needed. We had many great conversations on the work of the ministry and many wonderful stories of God's providence.

Before she passed away, she shared with me one incredible experience of God's providential intervention in protecting her from danger. After a full day of work, Mary made a final stop by the Patterson's vegetarian restaurant before heading home. The night was cold, and the wind began to pick up as she left the restaurant and headed to her car.

Along the way, Mary's car suddenly stalled and rolled right into the middle of the intersection in an area along 17th Street. Unfortunately, it was a notoriously dangerous, drug-infested area where she found herself deserted. It was 9:30 p.m. and very dark.

While sitting there stuck in her car helpless and alone, a number of impatient drivers blew their horns at her. Some people walked over as though they were going to help, but they just peaked through her window and stared at her. She did not have access to a phone to call for help, and she dreaded getting out of her car at that time of the night, especially in that part of town.

Strangers to the Rescue

As the time passed and the situation became more desperate, fear began to set in and ugly thoughts began to flash through her mind. As she contemplated on her dilemma, she claimed God's precious promises that He was her refuge and strength in time of trouble. She whispered an urgent prayer, "Lord, please help me!"

Almost instantly a pleasant young woman came to her car window. "Ms., would you like my mother to push you to the gas station?"

"Oh, yes, please!" said Mary. Her heart rejoiced at the prospect of getting to a place where she could get some help.

Disappointingly, as she reached to the gas station, she noticed that it was closed and to her inspecting eyes, there were a number of idle young men standing around like hungry predators waiting for prey. Quickly she called out to the young lady, "Miss, would you please ask your mother if she could push me from the gas station to my home on Sharswood Street?" The mother consented, and they started to push Mary towards her home.

Along the way, there were loud bangs from the rear as both bumpers occasionally made contact. As a result of the bumps and bangs, Mary thought that her car must have sustained substantial damage from those impacts that she felt.

Where Did They Go?

Finally, she approached her street, and as providence would have it, a parking space was conveniently available. With one final push from those unselfish strangers, her car rolled perfectly in the parking spot.

Excited and filled with gratitude, Mary hurriedly opened her door to express her thanks and appreciation to those kind and thoughtful people. But upon opening her door, there was no car or persons anywhere to be seen. The white car with mother and daughter simply vanished out of sight. "Where did they go?" Mary exclaimed. She stood there in absolute astonishment. "God must have sent His angels to help me out of trouble. Thank you, Jesus!" she shouted as she went into her house rejoicing and praising God.

"God is our refuge and strength, a very present help in trouble" (Ps. 46:1).

"Have not I commanded thee? Be strong and of a good courage; be not afraid, neither be thou dismayed: for the LORD thy God is with thee whither so ever thou goest" (Josh. 1:9).

"Be not forgetful to entertain strangers: for thereby some have entertained angels unawares" (Heb. 13:2).

Chapter Eleven

The Preacher Who Beats His Innocent Dog

It was a sunny summer day on August 3, 1987 when I went to an appointment to see a preacher by the name of Reverend Bullock. A few weeks earlier, his wife had bought the Bible on cassette tape from me, and he was impressed with them. He became interested in obtaining some books for himself, so we set a date for me to visit and show him the books and Bibles that I had.

Upon arriving at his home that day, I found him quite relaxed and sleeping on his front porch chair with his faithful dog laying by his feet.

Remembering how aggressive the dog was from my last visit, I stood back and called out to the preacher. "Reverend Bullock! Reverend Bullock!" There was no response from him because he was sound asleep. After not getting a response, I cautiously walked up the steps and gently knock on the porch gate. His dog did not seem alarmed and calmly got up and came towards me in a very friendly, unaggressive manner. Suddenly, Reverend Bullock awoke, and to his dismay, he saw his guard dog being very calm and friendly towards a stranger instead of presenting its normal growling and ready-to-pounce behavior.

He was enraged with his dog. He could not understand or come to grips with how his faithful watchdog did not alert him that a stranger had approached so close to his porch. In a fit of rage, he pulled the dog away, took it in the house, and began to beat it while repeatedly saying, "You are supposed to bite strangers, not greet them!" I could hear the growling of the dog as it was being beaten.

Anger Changes Things

The wise man Solomon was aware of the danger of being angry and has given us great counsels on the subject of anger.

"He that is slow to wrath is of great understanding: but he that is hasty of spirit exalteth folly" (Prov. 14:29).

"Be not hasty in thy spirit to be angry: for anger resteth in the bosom of fools" (Eccles. 7:9).

After beating his dog, Reverend Bullock came out to me, but he still had a look of anger and frustration on his face. He seemed speechless or perhaps a little ashamed of how he behaved. As he stood there in thoughtfulness, I deduced from his behavior that the incident had made a profound effect on his mood.

Knowing that he was a faithful minister of the gospel, I tried to reason with him from a spiritual perspective in an effort to try and mollify his anger. Smilingly, I said, "Reverend Bullock, don't you remember how God sent His angels to protect and deliver his servant, Daniel, from the ferocious lions?" But the reverend was reticent and did not respond to my question. Apparently, he was not in the frame of mind to reason any more that day, so he told me to come back at another time, which for some reason never materialized.

Another Preacher Who Beat His Animal

The incident with Reverend Bullock reminded me of the story of the prophet Balaam in Numbers 22. Balaam's uncontrolled anger caused him to beat his donkey abusively for not obeying his command. Little did he know that the animal was afraid to go forward because of an angel that was standing in the path. It was not until God opened Balaam's eyes that he was able to understand why the animal acted in such a strange, defiant manner.

> And when the ass saw the angel of the LORD, she fell down under Balaam: and Balaam's anger was kindled, and he smote the ass with a staff. And the LORD opened the mouth of the ass, and she said unto Balaam, What have I done unto thee, that thou hast smitten me these three times? (Num. 22:27, 28)

Here are the poignant words of the apostle Paul to the Ephesians: "Be ye angry, and sin not: let not the sun go down upon your wrath: Neither give place to the devil" (Eph. 4:26, 27). Many times, when I recall the story of the wailing dog, I often wondered how would it have played out if his dog was not involved in the situation. Would Reverend Bullock have bought the books? Only God knows. After thinking about Balaam's abusive act in beating his donkey compared with Reverend Bullock's abusive beating of his dog, there is another question that keeps lingering in my mind to this day. What would Reverend Bullock's dog have said to him had God opened its mouth to speak as he did with Balaam's donkey? Only God knows.

Chapter Twelve

Bread in the Briefcase

One night back in the early 1980s, when I was on my way home after seeing a customer, I felt that I was going to be the victim of a robbery. When walking alone at nights, I developed the habit of talking to the Lord in prayer along the way. I do this because you never know who or what you may encounter on the streets in my neighborhood, especially during the night.

On that night in question, I was nearing 60th and Spruce Street, a familiar intersection not far from my home. As I looked ahead, I noticed three young men who walked out of a bar and slowly in the direction that I was about to approach. I became curious because of the fact that they kept looking back at me. As I got close enough, I overheard one of them as he hinted to the others that that I might have some bread in my briefcase. I knew that they were speaking of me having money in my briefcase, so I became concerned and felt that I might be in for some possible hostile confrontation.

A Silent Prayer for Help

Without hesitation and in silence, I whispered an urgent prayer for divine help. Instantly, a strange feeling came over me. I felt as though I became taller and was walking on air. I also felt a sense of abnormal boldness and intrepidity as I had never felt before.

Feeling confident and unafraid, I kept on walking straight to where the three young men were standing as if waiting for me. As I approached them, I put my briefcase down in front of them and opened it. I then reached in, took out my Bible, held it out before them in confidence, and

> **I whispered an urgent prayer for divine help. Instantly, a strange feeling came over me. I felt as though I became taller and was walking on air.**

said, "Gentlemen, I overheard your conversation when you said that there was some bread in this briefcase. I want to let you know that you are absolutely right. This is the Bread of Life. Don't you know that Jesus is coming real soon, and He really wants to save you?"

The young men were stunned. One of them said to the others, "Come on, let's leave this guy alone." Hastily, two of them walked away, but one of them still stood before me frozen and speechless. With confidence, I spoke to him and said, "My friend, I am going to give you this little book called *Steps to Christ*. Please read it because it will really lead you to know more about Jesus, and next time you see me, please tell me how you enjoyed it." He took it from me and walked away to rejoin his two companions.

After they were gone, I stood there at the intersection giving thanks and praising God for sending His angels to guide and protect me in my time of urgent need. When I reached home, that wonderful feeling of boldness suddenly left me, and I was back to my old self. Suddenly, I started shaking when I realized what really happened. I could have been hurt, robbed, or even killed, but I thank God for His faithful promises that He will never leave us nor forsake us.

"Yea, though I walk through the valley of the shadow of death, I will fear no evil: for thou art with me; thy rod and thy staff they comfort me" (Ps. 23:4).

Chapter Thirteen

The Fifth Miracle at the Last Door

It was evening, and I was looking to make my last stop, so I went to see a gentleman who had sent in a response card requesting information on the children's Bible story books. The neighborhood he lived in was notorious for violence, and I really didn't want night to catch me there. As I knocked on the door and waited, I felt a little strange. After a couple minutes, I knocked again and was about to walk away when I heard the sound of the door being opened really slowly. Then I heard a man's voice asking, "Who are you?" As I looked, the first thing that caught my eye was a gun in his hand.

Immediately and without hesitation, I held out the lead card with his name and asked if he was the person who requested information about the Bible story books. After he said yes, I explained to him that I was there as a representative of the Family Health Education Service, and I had the information he had requested. After looking me up and down, he invited me into his home. I proceeded to enter, trusting that the angels of the Lord were with me to guide and protect me.

When I entered, I realized that he was in the process of cooking. He politely told me to take a seat at the table, but he still had a cautious look on his face and continued to hold the gun in his hand.

Finally, he put the gun down and told me to go ahead and say what I had to say. I then opened my briefcase, took out my prospectus, and began to give the canvas. He stood and listened. I showed him the Bible story books, and I explained all the features, the beautiful pictures and how easily it could be read and understood by every member of the family.

I pointed out how the Bible story could make lasting impression on children, how the heroes of the Bible become their role models. They grow in kindness, honesty, and courage. They learn to resist drugs, violence, and promiscuity and prepare children for a lifetime of making good decisions. I pointed out to him the scene of the second coming of Christ and ended on the importance of how the books help to prepare our children not just for this life but, more importantly, how we are to get ready to meet Jesus when He comes on the clouds of heaven.

He was quite impressed with the presentation, and I had a feeling that he was enjoying the canvas.

To my inspecting eyes, I saw no physical signs that there were children living in the house. Normally, I would ask how old are the children, but under the current circumstances, I did not feel impressed to ask too much questions. Anyway, I continued to explain the value and importance of the books. After my presentation, he said that he liked the books, but he was not prepared to get them at the time. He promised that he would get in touch with me when he was ready.

While I was about to leave, he offered me some of the meal he was preparing, but I told him that my wife was waiting for me to come home for dinner. I left his house with confidence knowing that the angels of God were with me. Sometimes we may never understand why God leads us in certain places, but as the Scriptures say, "Yea, though I walk through the valley of the shadow of death, I will fear no evil: for thou art with me; thy rod and thy staff they comfort me" (Ps. 23:4).

> "I planted the seed and left in God's capable hands to do as it seemed fit to Him."

We may never in this life see the fruits of our labor until the day when we stand on the sea of glass. Through the prophet Isaiah, God assures us, "Fear thou not; for I am with thee: be not dismayed; for I am thy God: I will strengthen thee; yea, I will help thee; yea, I will uphold thee with the right hand of my righteousness" (Isa. 41:10). I planted the seed and left in God's capable hands to do as it seemed fit to Him.

Chapter Fourteen

A Miracle at the Door

I Prayed While He Waved His Gun

In November 1980, there was a massive earthquake in California and Oregon that came to be called the Eureka earthquake. I remember watching the news on television but never gave much attention to it or felt its effect until a few days later while sitting down with an upset gentleman who pulled out a gun from his pocket.

When I knocked on the door of an elderly man on Walnut Street in West Philadelphia, he was very polite as he invited me into his home. The atmosphere of his home felt very tranquil, and he seemed to be quite congenial and easygoing. After he offered me to take a seat, we had a brief, jovial conversation, after which I reaffirmed the purpose of my visit and began to present my canvas. However, during the course of my presentation, he suddenly became emotional and started to cry as he talked about his daughter in California whom he had not heard from since the news of the then recent earthquake.

I tried to console him, but he became even more emotional. He reached into his pocket, pulled out a gun, and kept saying, "I don't know what I am going to do." He kept on repeating it while waving the gun around.

A Moment to Decide

At that critical moment, I thought that he might do harm to himself and perhaps to me as well, even though he didn't point the gun directly at me or himself. I was in a dilemma and didn't know what to do or say to mollify his feelings. My only recourse was to whisper a silent prayer and talk to him about the love of Jesus. I encouraged him not to worry and reassured him that God would allow his daughter to contact him soon.

I was extremely nervous at first, but he suddenly calmed down and immediately put me at ease. It was only through the power of the Holy Spirit and the influence of the ministering angels of God that his anger was assuaged. Thankfully, there was peace above the storm. I was able to leave him a small book, *Steps to Christ*, and finally said goodbye in peace.

"Why should the sons and daughters of God be reluctant to pray, when prayer is the key in the hand of faith to unlock heaven's storehouse, where are treasured the boundless resources of Omnipotence?" (White, *Steps to Christ*, p. 94).

The lesson I learned was that I must put my trust in God no matter what the situation may be. The Bible says: "Wait on the LORD: be of good courage, and he shall strengthen thine heart: wait, I say, on the LORD" (Ps. 27:14).

Also, in Joshua 1:9, it says: "Have not I commanded thee? Be strong and of a good courage; be not afraid, neither be thou dismayed: for the LORD thy God is with thee whithersoever thou goest."

Who knows? It may be that that gentleman might have been planning to take his life. Perhaps my mission to knock on his door that day was to administer to his needs in bringing him peace of mind and encouragement. My sincere hope is that when Jesus comes, I will be able to greet that gentleman again on our way to the glorious city of God, the New Jerusalem.

> God will impress those whose hearts are open to truth, and who are longing for guidance. He will say to His human agent, "Speak to this one or to that one of the love of Jesus." No sooner is the name of Jesus mentioned in love and tenderness than angels of God draw near, to soften and subdue the heart. (White, *Colporteur Ministry*, p.111)

Chapter Fifteen

Another Miracle at the Door

From Disappointment to Joy

It so happened that one Sunday morning I went out to put brochures advertising books north of Market Street in West Philadelphia. After a few hours in the process of putting out hundreds of them, I suddenly discovered one brochure that was left on a porch from one of my fellow colleagues. I realized that the two of us were working in the same territory. Naturally, I became concerned because I did not want to waste precious material, time, energy, and fruitless efforts.

In order to get some direction on how to solve the problem, I called my associate leader at the time, Sister Bea Johnson, and explained the territory assignment situation. To my surprise, all she said was, "Brother Devon, don't worry about it. Keep on advertising. The Lord is going to bless you regardless." With that being said, I took her advice and continued to work and advertise in the area. Within a few days, I received a lead card that came from a lady within that same area. She was requesting information on the Bible stories and the Bible reference library set.

That day when I knocked on the prospect's door, I was stunned and flabbergasted to find out that it was Yvonne, someone I knew from my high school years; we had both worked at the same institution as part-time employees.

"I remember you!" she said when she opened her door. "We worked at the same place some years ago. Come on in, and let's talk."

It was such a joy to enter her home and reminisce. I was able to meet her young son and daughter for whom she was very eager to get the books.

Following our conversation, she happily placed an order for the Bible story books for her children as well as books for herself.

However, my greatest delight was not the sale of the books; it was their surprise decision to take Bible studies. Without hesitation, I immediately turned their names over to the Bible worker to start the studies. How wonderful it was that at the end of the Bible studies, Yvonne and her two children gave their lives to the Lord and were baptized as brand-new members of the remnant church. What a great lesson to learn! So often, what may seem to us as a huge disappointment turns out be a most wonderful blessing.

"And we know that all things work together for good to them that love God, to them who are the called according to his purpose" (Rom. 8:28).

"And the lord said unto the servant, Go out into the highways and hedges, and compel them to come in, that my house may be filled" (Luke 14:23).

Chapter Sixteen

Are You Going to Break Down My Door, Sir?

Despite being very new to literature work in the 1970s, I had been trained on how to politely approach people and also how to discreetly and correctly knock on someone's door. The area assigned for me to work was not far from where I was living, which made things very convenient for me because I did not have transportation at the time.

One evening while many people were sitting out and enjoying the summer weather, I began working in the cool of the day. Because of this, I had the opportunity to meet people while they were sitting on their porches. As I made my way down the block, I came to a door and knocked. When there was no response, I knocked a second time. Then a man with a very boisterous voice emerged and shouted at me loud enough that all his neighbors could hear him.

"Are you going to break down my door sir?" he shouted. It seemed that he wanted to make a show to his neighbors. I thought the manner in which he acted was very arrogant, and I got the impression that his neighbors knew him to be of that nature. It was quite evident that I would not be able to hold a meaningful conversation with him, so I quietly moved on to the next door, leaving him to cogitate on his rude behavior.

The Other Side of the Street

In contrast, on the other side of the street, I met a very nice family: Bishop Stevenson and his wife, Evangelist Stevenson, along with their grandchildren. They were very warm and friendly people. They decided to purchase some of my books, including a regular large print Bible for the family. While doing my presentation, Evangelist became concerned about the pictures of the four beasts as described in the prophecy of Daniel 7 and also the beast with the seven heads and ten horns and two-horned beasts of Revelation 13.

She exclaimed, "No, no! I don't want to see those pictures. Those are the terrible things that are going to come upon the earth." From her comments, I deduced that her knowledge concerning the meaning of the symbolic beasts was limited. She was not aware that the two-horned beast of Revelation 13 was, in actuality, the symbol of the United States of America, the very country in which she was living.

As I endeavored to explain the meaning of those prophetic symbols, Evangelist shouted, "You are a prophet!" From that day onward, she would refer to me as prophet Devon. Through my contact with the Stevenson family, I was able to make sales to other members of their congregation.

One day, while visiting their home, I asked Bishop and Evangelist about the prospect of me giving Bible studies at their church since they showed an interest in the prophesies of Daniel and also Revelation. They agreed, and it was arranged for the study to be conducted on Tuesday evenings at their regular scheduled prayer meeting time. Assisting me with the studies was one of my fellow literature evangelists, Brother Trawick.

What a contrast between the Stevenson's home and the boisterous and intimidating neighbor across the street. In our work for Christ, we are going come across people who are not very kind, and the Bible warns us about that. "Blessed are ye, when men shall revile you, and persecute you, and shall say all manner of evil against you falsely, for my sake. Rejoice, and be exceeding glad: for great is your reward in heaven: for so persecuted they the prophets which were before you" (Matt. 5:11, 12).

> **In our work for Christ, we are going come across people who are not very kind, and the Bible warns us about that.**

We will meet people like Nabal, a churlish and evil man in 2 Samuel 25, who showed no respect or gratitude to King David and his men after they had done so much to protect his assets. But the Bible tells how to feel about people like this. "Be not afraid of their faces: for I am with thee to deliver thee, saith the LORD" (Jer. 1:8). "And thou, son of man, be not afraid of them, neither be afraid of their words, though briers and thorns be with thee, and thou dost dwell among scorpions: be not afraid of their words, nor be dismayed at their looks, though they be a rebellious house" (Ezek. 2:6).

The Stevenson's Church

On the opening night of the Bible study, Brother Trawick and I sat quietly and observed the preliminary part of the service. There were only two musical instruments that were used: a piano and a set of drums. As the music played, the members clapped, sang, danced, and shouted in tongues. Finally, as the music calmed down, my friend and I were introduced.

As I stood and began the Bible study, there was a good degree of attentiveness, but as we got into the meat of the study, it became very evident to me that it was not as exciting as the dancing, shouting, and speaking in tongues. Some of the members, perhaps exhausted from the first part of the service, began to doze away during the study. However, at the end of the study when the drums and the piano started to play, it was amazing to see how quickly the members jumped to their feet and began to dance and shout again.

Unfortunately, because of building problems and other factors, we were not able to continue the studies as planned. However, I kept up with the Stevenson family for some time after. I am ever mindful of the fact that we wrestle not against flesh and blood. "Lest Satan should get an advantage of us: for we are not ignorant of his devices" (2 Cor. 2:11). Only eternity will be able to reveal what impact that first study may have had that night at the Stevenson's church.

Chapter Seventeen

Yet Another Miracle at the Door

From Anger to Joy

One summer evening as I went out doing my literature work, a very good friend and church brother, Enoch Baker, accompanied me. He had heard so many positive testimonies about the literature work that he wanted to experience firsthand how the work was done.

As we walked along the way, we talked about God's goodness. Finally, we entered a little street, and I started knocking on doors. As we were about to approach her porch, we noticed the lady who lived there as well as her children had decided to come out of the house and sit on the porch. As we reached her steps, she beat us to the punch by preemptively stating, "Please don't even bother to talk to me. I am tired; I am frustrated; I am angry, and I don't need anyone aggravating me."

Unable to think of anything to say, I was momentarily lost for words, but a thought came into my mind on how I should respond to her. "I am truly sorry about your situation, Miss. I can see that you are tired and frustrated and angry and upset. But I am a friend in the community, and I only wanted to talk to you for just a brief moment." After saying those words to her, her aggressive attitude seemed assuaged and in a peaceful manner, she looked at us and agreed to speak with us for just a few minutes.

Her porch was very tiny and did not have enough room for much accommodation, so my friend and I stepped up on the porch, and while I sat down and gave a brief presentation on the Bible story books, he stood and prayed silently for me and her.

During the presentation, I felt a wonderful peace as I shared the love of Jesus with her. I spoke of how He calmed the raging Sea of Galilee in the storm and how He died for us. As I looked at her face, she seemed so transformed. All the frustration, anxiety, and anger that she had displayed was replaced with a radiant smile and watery eyes. Time was no longer of concern, as she began to open up to us and shared the reason why she had reacted in such an unfriendly manner as she did.

"I am so glad that you stopped by today. The reason why I responded the way I did was because my mother is in the hospital. My sister is also in the hospital, and my best friend is in the hospital as well. With all of that on my mind, I was feeling very despondent. But thank God you stopped by. I want those books for my children. How much are they?" When I told her the price, she asked if I would accept a check as a down payment. We rejoiced and prayed with her before we left. Subsequently she was enrolled in a Bible correspondence course.

That evening was an experience that I will never forget. In every encounter I have had, there was always a wonderful lesson to be learned. What I had learned from that particular occasion was that when we are lost for words, we should just put our trust in God. He will know what to say in the time of need. For Jesus can read the hearts of those people, and He knows just what it takes to subdue those hearts.

This is the counsel that Jesus gave to His disciples. "And when they bring you unto the synagogues, and unto magistrates, and powers, take ye no thought how or what thing ye shall answer, or what ye shall say: For the Holy Ghost shall teach you in the same hour what ye ought to say" (Luke 12:11, 12).

Even though we have lost contact over the years, my hope is that we will be able to reunite when Jesus comes again. For the time being, I will never forget that transforming miracle at the door.

The story did not end right there. It extended to the joy of meeting her mother.

Laughter Is Good for the Soul

It is so strange the way things happens sometimes, and that is why many people often quote this special verse: "And we know that all things work together for good to them that love God, to them who are the called according to his purpose" (Rom. 8:28).

When the young lady's mother was discharged from the hospital, I visited her because of her interest in the medical books. While sitting and talking with her in her home, I noticed a strange picture hanging on the wall of her living room. It was a picture of a convertible car with Jesus in the driver's seat and a man and woman sitting in the rear seats. I was curious to know who drew the picture and the meaning behind it. I sat and listened eagerly as she began to explain. She told me that the picture was the work of her grandson. The man and woman sitting in the back seats of the car were Adam and Eve, and the reason why Jesus was sitting around the steering wheel was because he was driving them out of the garden of Eden. Wow! It was so hysterical that I could not hold back and burst out in laughter.

"Then was our mouth filled with laughter, and our tongue with singing: then said they among the heathen, The LORD hath done great things for them" (Ps. 126:2).

"A merry heart doeth good like a medicine: but a broken spirit drieth the bones" (Prov. 17:22).

On the other hand, it showed that her grandson had a brilliant imagination, amazing talent, and great insight. While children may look at things literally from their perspective, we can always learn a lesson from their innocence.

Pictures Are Worth More

One of the reasons why we highlight the colorful pictures in the Bible story books to parents is to emphasize how a picture is worth more than a thousand words. Because children remember more of what they see than what they hear, it is highly important that parents know what their children read and what they watch on television, tablets, or smart phones. Some unmonitored programs could permanently leave a baneful effect on their characters.

However, whoever we are, male or female, black or white, God respects our choices and whatever we chose to believe in. He never coerces or forces anyone against their will. "He that loveth not knoweth not God; for God is love" (1 John 4:8).

"I Never Want Any of My Children to Look upon That Jew!"

During World War II in Nazi Germany, hatred for Jews knew no bounds.

Carl Benz simply loathed the sight of a Jew. He declared, "I never want any of my children to ever have to look upon a Jew."

His pregnant wife was eventually driven to hospital, where, in the maternity ward, she was put in a one-bed room.

Carl Benz went to visit his wife, as she lay, waiting for the event. Casting his eyes around the room, he noticed a picture on the wall. It was a picture of Jesus Christ. The blood flushed to his face. He began to shake. In a rage, he rushed to the sister-in-charge. "What is that picture of a Jew doing in my wife's room?" He demanded.

"I cannot remove it, sir"

"Do you hear me?" he roared. "I never want any of my children to look upon that Jew!" They did not remove it. A few hours later, his child was born. It was a boy. But it did not ever have to look upon that picture of a Jew. That baby was born blind. (Gray, *Ark of the Covenant*, p. 225)

"I will set no wicked thing before mine eyes: I hate the work of them that turn aside; it shall not cleave to me" (Ps. 101:3).

"Keep thy heart with all diligence; for out of it are the issues of life" (Prov. 4:23).

"All should guard the senses, lest Satan gain victory over them; for these are the avenues of the soul" (White, *Counsels for the Church*, p. 166).

Jesus desired His disciples to learn a lesson from children and that's the reason He said, "...Suffer little children, and forbid them not, to come unto me: for of such is the kingdom of heaven" (Matt. 19:14).

"Finally, brethren, whatsoever things are true, whatsoever things are honest, whatsoever things are just, whatsoever things are pure, whatsoever things are lovely, whatsoever things are of good report; if there be any virtue, and if there be any praise, think on these things" (Phil. 4:8).

The Reason That I Sell Bible and Bedtime Story Books

As we look around the world today, it seems as if it is falling apart on every side. Our children are tomorrow's future, and with an inundation of social media, bad associations, and a lack of spiritual training, many of our children may go in the wrong direction. We are also living in a permissive society, and the danger is that children who live in permissive households may also learn behaviors that do not serve them well as they grow older.

Fiction vs. Truth

While children are familiar with Winnie-the-Pooh, Daffy Duck, Fred Flintstone, Bugs Bunny, Mickey Mouse, and more, many of them are not familiar with the heroes of the Bible.

On one occasion when I was making a presentation on the Bible story books, I asked a little boy by the name of David what he wanted to be when he grew up. His response was that he wanted to be Superman. Thank God that his parents saw the values of the books and made an investment in the Bible story set for their son.

Here is where the Bible and bedtime story books make a difference. These stories teach life's most valuable lessons. They make a lasting impression on children. The heroes of the Bible become their role models. They grow in kindness, honesty, and courage. They learn to resist drugs, violence, and promiscuity. The books bring out the best in our children and are a great way to prepare them for a lifetime of making good decisions.

I am very grateful to God that I saw the need and personally invested in those wonderful books for my own children at an early age. Their spiritual maturity today is a direct result from the influence of the heroes of the Bible.

"Train up a child in the way he should go: and when he is old, he will not depart from it" (Prov. 22:6).

The Reason That I Sell Bible and Bedtime Story Books

As we look around the world today, it seems as if it is falling apart on every side. Our children are tomorrow's future, and with an inundation of social media, bad associations, and a lack of spiritual training, many of our children may go in the wrong direction. We are also living in a permissive society, and the danger is that children who live in permissive households may also learn behaviors that do not serve them well as they grow older.

Fiction vs. Truth

While children are familiar with Winnie-the-Pooh, Daffy Duck, Fred Flintstone, Bugs Bunny, Mickey Mouse, and more, many of them are not familiar with the heroes of the Bible.

On one occasion when I was making a presentation on the Bible story books, I asked a little boy by the name of David what he wanted to be when he grew up. His response was that he wanted to be Superman. Thank God that his parents saw the values of the books and made an investment in the Bible story set for their son.

Here is where the Bible and bedtime story books make a difference. These stories teach life's most valuable lessons. They make a lasting impression on children. The heroes of the Bible become their role models. They grow in kindness, honesty, and courage. They learn to resist drugs, violence, and promiscuity. The books bring out the best in our children and are a great way to prepare them for a lifetime of making good decisions.

I am very grateful to God that I saw the need and personally invested in those wonderful books for my own children at an early age. Their spiritual maturity today is a direct result from the influence of the heroes of the Bible.

"Train up a child in the way he should go: and when he is old, he will not depart from it" (Prov. 22:6).

Chapter Eighteen

In Plain Sight but Not Seen

One day, I decided to knock on the door of Mary Facey, an elderly friend of the family. When she opened her door and saw that it was me, she was overjoyed and gladly invited me in. After talking for a while, I showed her the Bible reference books, and she decided to get the set of books right away. She decided to make a down payment of $100. After I wrote up the contract, she went for the money but could not find it. She looked at all the places she thought she could have placed it but to no avail. Finally, I suggested that we pray about it and then, by faith, she would go and look one more time.

After the prayer, she went to look, and lo and behold, it was right at the place where she had already looked. She could not figure out how she had missed it. I believe that there is always a good reason why God allows certain things to happen in our life. Sometimes it may be that God wants to teach us valuable lessons that we might not have learned otherwise. "And we know that all things work together for good to them that love God, to them who are the called according to his purpose" (Rom. 8:28).

Chapter Nineteen

The Sixth Miracle at the Last Door

Please Leave My House

One beautiful summer day, while working on a busy street selling small books and magazines, I met a very delightful young lady named Casandra. She went by Sandra for short. While glancing through some of my magazines, she became interested in the one that shows people how to stop smoking. She had no funds on her at the time in order to purchase the magazine, so she invited me to pay a visit to her home to pick up the payment. She also wanted me to show her some of the other books that I had mentioned.

The day finally came, and I went to her home. When I knocked on the door, her brother, Ryan, answered to see who it was, and after I explained who I was and that I had come to see his sister, he invited me in. I entered the house through a haze of cigarette smoke and a noticeable scent of alcohol. Present were Mrs. Shay, Sandra, her brother, and an elderly man who was a friend of the family.

Sandra invited me to sit in the dining room where it would be more convenient for me to show her the books. While I was giving the canvas, Sandra asked me to elaborate on the larger spiritual books, so I began to explain. Before I could finish my presentation, Mrs. Shay walked into the dining and upon hearing the conversation became very hostile towards me, and with a few angry expletives, she told me to pack up my books and leave her house. "I don't want anyone coming into my house talking about God and the Bible," she said.

From the tone of her voice and the look on her countenance, it was obvious to me that she was inebriated. Seeing that I was not welcome in her home, I politely made my exit, as Sandra apologized for her mother's ill-mannered behavior. While I was walking away from her home, I prayed and asked God to bless her in spite of her behavior.

The devil thought he had gained a victory that night by chasing me away, but he was in for a big shock. What happened next is so miraculous, so awesome, so thrilling, so captivating, that you won't believe it. God was going to turn that negative event around to His own glory.

One Year Later

About one year later as I was passing by their street, I saw Mrs. Shay's son sitting on the doorsteps enjoying a cigarette. I seized upon the opportunity, and I went over to talk with him. He was a very eloquent and intelligent young man.

During the course of our conversation, the evening had gotten darker and the stars came out, so I engaged him in a talk on astronomy. When I saw that he had an interest in that subject, I linked it to the Bible and mentioned how angels travel faster than the speed of light. He did not believe me that it was in the Bible, so I referred him to Daniel 9. There in that chapter the prophet was praying about a matter that he did not clearly understand. While he was praying, the angel Gabriel left the courts of heaven, billions of lightyears away, and came quickly to Daniel to deliver the answer that he was seeking before he could finish his prayer.

"Wow!" exclaimed Ryan. He was amazed that the Bible could sound so interesting. As a result of his interest, we continued our conversation for a couple more hours. Eventually, I told him that I had to go because I had to be at church early the next morning. He was very curious as to why I would be going to church on a Saturday.

The following Friday evening as I was again passing by, I saw Ryan once again sitting on his doorstep, so I wasted no time. I went over to him and I started talking about some other interesting subject in the Bible.

The Big Shock

Surprisingly, and unknown to me or Ryan, his mother was sitting close to the window and listening to everything that I was sharing with her son.

Finally, she could not hold her peace any longer and asked me if I was the young man that came to the house selling books about a year ago.

Suspensefully, I answered with a degree of apprehension, not knowing whether she would once again ask me to leave. However, to my shock, her reaction turned out to be a very pleasant and unexpected surprise.

Excitedly, she explained to me that the things that I was sharing with her son sounded very interesting and that she was greatly impressed and would like to learn more about the Bible, too. She invited me to come inside her house and share the Bible with her. I could hardly believe my ears as I pondered the obvious question. How could the same person who angrily chased me from her home now lovingly entreat me to come into her home? With joy, I went inside and after sharing some of the beautiful passages of the Bible, she urged me come back and study with her and her family. I then told her that if she had friends and relatives who were interested, she could invite them as well.

The Bible Study

There was much fun and excitement studying the Bible with Mrs. Shay and her family. When we studied about the prophecy of the image of Daniel 2, Sandra saw the awesome and fascinating foreknowledge of God in accurately predicting the rise and fall of kingdoms from 606 BC to the end of time. Overjoyed with the overwhelming sweetness of God's Word, she invited a few of her friends, so they could also see the beauty in studying the Word of God.

When Mrs. Shay discovered that her loved ones who had passed away were not able to communicate with those who are living and that such communication was the deception of the devil and his evil angels, she was shocked.

Her son was a very studious young man and well-read. As we delved into study of the prophecy of Daniel 7 about the four great beasts and the little horn, he was blown away when he learned that it was not God who changed the day of worship, but it was the little horn power. He saw the historical fact that on March 7, 321, Roman Emperor Constantine 1 issued a civil decree making Sunday a day of rest from labor. He stated, "All judges and city people and craftsmen shall rest upon the venerable day of the sun." It was truly a shocker to them all.

An Astounding Transformation

The Bible study was truly enjoyable and lasted almost a year. With the wealth of new information they had discovered from diligently studying the Bible, they were totally convinced and convicted by the truthfulness of the unadulterated and infallible word of God.

As we studied about the body temple and how we should present our bodies to God as a living sacrifice, they were convicted and through the power of the Holy Spirit, they gave up drinking, smoking, and other health-destroying habits. The transformation was truly a born-again experience.

The conclusion was a remarkable turn of events. Who would believe that same lady who drove me out of the house and did not want anything to do with God would accept Jesus Christ as her personal Lord and Savior? Ryan also fell in love with Jesus and decided that he would follow in His footsteps and regularly go to church on the Sabbath day.

The Baptism

How beautiful it was on that Sabbath day to see both mother and son as they went down into the watery grave of baptism and became new members of God's remnant church. Sometime after her mother and brother's baptism, Sandra attended church one Sabbath. She was so impressed and convicted that she took her stand to be baptized. But somehow, instead of following through with her conviction to get baptized, she procrastinated. She was encouraged many times to surrender her life to Jesus and get baptized, but she said that she was not ready right then and that she would one day soon. She had good intentions.

An Untimely Death

It was devastating when I was told the heartbreaking news that Sandra had suddenly passed. It was a huge and unexpected shock to everyone. She was only about thirty years old and just beginning to enjoy life. My heart was broken and wounded at her sudden and mysterious passing. She was a very pleasant and loving person with a winsome and gregarious personality. Why did that happen to her? God only knows.

How could I forget the day I met her on the street and introduced her to the *How to Stop Smoking* magazine. It was Sandra who introduced me to her family. Of all the people, I honestly thought that she would have been the first one to be baptized. That experience with the Shay family was both a bitter and sweet one.

What did I learn from that experience? I have learned that even though people may be angry and furious with you, even though they abuse you and chase you away, as Mrs. Shay did, we should never give up on them. God never gives up on us because, with God, all things are possible.

Often times, we may become discouraged along the way, but thank God we have the Holy Scriptures that bring comfort and encouragement to our hearts. I am reminded of Psalm 43:5, "Why art thou cast down, O my soul? and why art thou disquieted within me? hope in God: for I shall yet praise him, who is the health of my countenance, and my God."

I am grateful to God for the experiences through which He has brought me. In all my trials, all my joy and all my sorrows, prayer is always the answer. The apostle Paul reminds us:

> Who shall separate us from the love of Christ? shall tribulation, or distress, or persecution, or famine, or nakedness, or peril, or sword? As it is written, For thy sake we are killed all the day long; we are accounted as sheep for the slaughter. Nay, in all these things we are more than conquerors through him that loved us. (Rom. 8:35–37)

In one of the favorite books that I sell, it says, "The gospel is to be carried forward by aggressive warfare, in the midst of opposition, peril, loss, and suffering. But those who do this work are only following in their Master's steps" (White, *The Desire of Ages*, p. 678)

Chapter Twenty

The Book That Turned a Church 180 Degrees

One of the eye-opening books that literature evangelists sell is called, *The Triumph of God's Love*, otherwise known as *The Great Controversy*. Its contents illuminate the pages of the Bible in such a lucid way that it enables the reader to understand, enjoy, and see the Bible like they have never seen it before.

In a story I've heard told by Brother Roy Dennis, a Pentecostal pastor was given a copy of *The Great Controversy*. After having read the book completely, he was convinced of the truth about the Sabbath. Under the conviction of the Holy Spirit, the next sermon that he preached to his sixty-member congregation was about the seventh-day Sabbath. Following his sermon, the congregation affirmed his presentation with a hearty amen with the exception of two families of a deacon and an elder, who got up and left after the sermon. Following that, all the remaining members were given a copy of *The Great Controversy*. Today, they are now a happy Sabbath-keeping Christian congregation. All because of that one amazing book.

He Stole a Book

In a book called *They Walk with Angels*, William Higgins talks about a young man who lived in Guyana who was determined to be a spiritualist (p. 97). He was sure that being one would help him to become rich quickly, so he set out to obtain books with instruction he needed to become a successful spiritualist.

One day he went to see his uncle, who showed him a book he had recently bought and kept in the bottom of his trunk. As the young man looked through it, he noticed a chapter entitled, "Spiritualism," and decided to obtain the book by whatever means were necessary. Convinced that his uncle would not lend it to him, and not knowing where he could obtain a copy for himself, he decided to steal it.

During the night the young man sneaked into his uncle's house and stole the book. The book was *The Great Controversy*. He began reading it that very night, starting at the chapter that held special interest. The more he read, the more he saw the truth about spiritualism. He went right back and read the chapter a second time. He then read the five chapters beginning with "The Origin of Evil," to and including, "The First Great Deception."

The truth of what he read gripped his heart, and he ended up reading the entire book. Having completed it, he decided to become a Seventh-day Adventist. But what about the stolen book? He decided there was only one thing to do: go to his uncle, confess his wrong, and return the book. This he did. In his confession he told the uncle how sorry he was that he stole the book, yet how glad he was that he had taken it and read it because in it he had found God's truth and had been saved from Satan's snare.

Chapter Twenty-One

The Fourth Miracle at the Door

When I moved into my new home on the 700 block of Wynnewood Road in Philadelphia, I knocked on every door of my neighbors' homes selling books. They got to know we were a Christian family really quickly.

At one point when we had church in our home, our neighbor got to know us even better, especially when members gathered on the porch on Sabbath evenings to sing. Many of the neighbors would come out on their porches to listen and enjoy the singing. These experiences were a part of the factor in helping our neighbors develop great respect for us.

On a Sabbath afternoon in July 1998, my family and I had just return from church when one of my neighbors, a brother, called out to me in urgency. "Mr. Roberts, my wife would like to speak with you."

"Ok, no problem. As soon as I help take my daughter in the house, I will come over to see her," I said. While my wife was getting lunch on the table, I hurriedly walked to my neighbor to see what it was all about.

Preventing Potential Violence

On my way to the house, my heart was filled with suspense and curiosity as to the urgency. When I knocked on the door, Ms. Adreene kindly invited me to take a seat. Observing from her gesture, tone of voice, and visage, I knew that she was emotionally upset. As I tactfully tried to ascertain the reason that she wanting to talk with me, she reminded me of a concern that she had expressed to me in an earlier conversation months earlier. In that conversation, she spoke about strange people on our street. At that time, she did not exactly explain what she meant, but I had made a note of the conversation in my prayer journal, dated January 8, 1998, when she first mentioned it.

As I sat and talked with her, she told me that something terrible was going to go down on the street between her and another neighbor. She stated emphatically that it was not going to be pretty. "Mr. Roberts, I just wanted you and your wife to know about it before it happens because I have great respect for you both," she said.

With sincere neighborly concern, I asked her what could be so bad that would cause her to resort to such violent confrontation. She explained that she was upset that a certain neighbor was saying all manner of negative things about her to other neighbors on the block. She said that it had reached the point that in order to stop it, she was going to do something violent.

I told her that it was God who in His love and mercy impressed the desire upon her heart to reach out to me. When I said that to her, she blurted, "God doesn't care about me. That's why I took all my Bibles and threw then in the trash." Hearing that, I tried to reassure her how loving and caring God was, and the very fact that I was there talking to her was an indication that He sent me to reassure her of that fact. I then asked her if she would mind me offering up a word of prayer with her, and she consented.

While I was praying with her, she wept bitterly as tears ran down her face, and I truly sensed that burdens were being lifted from her heart. After the prayer, her face which was fraught with worry and pain was transformed into a resplendent smile. "I really appreciate that, Mr. Roberts. Thank you so much for caring. I feel much better."

Before I left, I asked her if she would mind me having a talk with our neighbor about the matter. She gladly said that it would be fine with her. As I left her home that afternoon, my prayer was that God would intervene in some way to obviate any hostile confrontation.

Meeting with the Neighbor

The neighbor in question was a very caring and loving Christian person, and we get along very well. After speaking together about the situation, my neighbor was very shocked and surprised at such a thought and was not aware of saying anything that could have agitated another neighbor to the point of being so angry and upset. As Christians, we both knew that regardless of what the circumstance may be, it was the machination of the power of darkness trying to disrupt the peace and unity among good neighbors. Therefore, we prayed together that whatever the devil's invidious intent may be, we would leave the matter in God's capable hands.

Eventually, through the power of God's divine intervention, the devil's scheme to disrupt the peace and harmony on the block was defeated, and that hostile confrontation was totally averted.

"Behold, I give unto you power to tread on serpents and scorpions, and over all the power of the enemy: and nothing shall by any means hurt you" (Luke 10:19).

The Story Continues

The following Sabbath when I returned from church, I saw Ms. Adreene sitting on her steps. I was impressed to take her a little book called *Steps to Christ*, so I handed it to her and told her that God impressed me to share it with her, and she gladly received it.

In that little book it talks about God's love for humanity, a sinner's need of Christ, repentance, confession, the privilege of prayer, and much more. For me, personally, that same little book has helped me to experience the incredible power of prayer. That is the main reason why I keep a prayer journal. It reminds me of the prayers that God has answered in the past, and at the same time, it builds my confidence and hope that He is the same yesterday, today, tomorrow, and forever.

An Unexpected Check for a Thousand Dollars

Two weeks or so after talking, praying, and sharing the book with Ms. Adreene, my wife and I were in the kitchen when we heard a sound coming from the mailbox. At the time, we were washing, drying, and putting away dishes. We wondered what it was since it was too late for mail delivery. Out of curiosity, I quickly went to the door to find an envelope. I took it to the kitchen so Cynthia and I could check it out. When we opened it, we saw that it was a thank you card from Ms. Adreene. She was thanking us for being kind and caring neighbors.

However, the bigger surprise was a smaller sealed envelope within the thank you card. *Why another envelope?* we asked ourselves. Filled with suspense, we finally opened it and saw a note and a check. The note read, "Thank you, Mr. Roberts, for taking the time to come over and talk with me. It was really appreciated. I hope this will help you get a computer." It was a check for one thousand dollars.

How Did She Know?

We needed an additional $1000 exactly to afford a computer. She did not know that, but God knew it. In retrospect, I remembered a day while she was working on her flower garden in the front yard, and I went over and complimented her. During the course of that conversation, we covered a few subjects, one of which was about computers. At the time, she had asked me if I had owned one, and my reply was no.

My 1979 Covenant

I made a covenant with God back in 1979, and one of my pledges was to be a faithful steward in tithes and offerings. During that period of time when I received the check for a $1000, I was the only bread winner in my home. We had two young children, one of which had disabilities that required my wife to be a stay-at-home mom. When it comes to returning tithes and offerings, Cynthia and I are very faithful. It was a part of our baptismal vows that we made before we were baptized. It is our practice that before we pay any of our bills, our tithes and offerings are taken out first, and whatever is left over goes toward the bills. We pledged to put God first in everything we do, and not once did He ever fail to provide for us. "But seek ye first the kingdom of God, and his righteousness; and all these things shall be added unto you" (Matt. 6:33).

We Were in Need

That month when we received that check, we were not able to meet all of our expenses because we were one thousand dollars short. Cynthia asked, "What are we going to do, honey?" My reply was that we have done what God has asked us to do, so we will rely upon His promise in Malachi 3:10, "Bring ye all the tithes into the storehouse, that there may be meat in mine house, and prove me now herewith, saith the LORD of hosts, if I will not open you the windows of heaven, and pour you out a blessing, that there shall not be room enough to receive it."

Not a Penny More, Not a Penny Less

We presented our concerns to God in prayer and trusted in His word. When we received that check of the exact amount that day, we knew that it was an answer to our prayer. Was it coincidental? Not at all, because the next time we fell short of $1,100 in our bills, we had a visit from my mother, Ada, and her twin sister, Aunt Sweetie, as I call her. While Cynthia and I were conversing with them, they handed us two envelopes, one from my mother and the other from my aunt. When we opened the envelopes and counted the money, it was exactly $1,100. Not a penny more and not a penny less. Was it coincidental? Not at all, because the next time when I needed exactly $500, God provided it. Not a penny more, not a penny less.

In that situation, I was at work when Cynthia called to give me the good news. "Honey, guess what? You wouldn't believe it." Jenny, her sister, had just dropped off $500. It was unbelievable because that's exactly the amount that we needed. Jenny did not know that we were in need of that exact amount of money, but God knew our needs and spoke to her generous heart, and she acted on it. Was it coincidental? Not at all, because the next time that we needed just fifty cents, it was miraculously provided during the night while we were asleep.

A Fifty Cent Miracle

During those times, I took public transportation to work. That night before I went to bed, I realized that I was short fifty cents to get a transfer from one bus to the other. I searched to see if I could find some pennies laying around the house to make up the bus fare, but I came up empty. I asked my wife if she had any coins anywhere, but she could not find any. So, I decided that would wake up real early and walk to work. Once I made it, I could always walk home no matter how long it would take. I prayed and went to bed, having my mind made up.

In the morning, to my surprise, there were two quarters laying on my dresser, and I was quite sure that it was my wife who placed them there while I was asleep. Because I didn't want to wake her, I waited until I reached work to call and thank her for the change. When I called and expressed my thanks, she swore that she didn't put it there. Where did it come from? Was it coincidental? Not at all. I could go on and on, but let's think about it for a moment. If Jesus could use two fish and five barley loaves to feed more than five thousand people, surely, He could provide fifty cents for me. Don't you think so?

On another occasion, we were in dire need of diapers for our children but had no money to purchase them because of hard times. My wife and I prayed about the matter and left it in God's hands.

Rechecking Wedding Gift Envelopes

Even though we had previously gone through all our wedding gifts two years before, the thought came to me to go back and check through all the envelopes again, just in case we may have overlooked opening any or that perhaps God through His foreknowledge withheld our eyes from seeing one of them until we were in dire need. Thank God that we did not throw them away.

One by one, I rechecked with the hope that, somehow, I would find something. Amazingly, I found one envelop with enough cash to buy the diapers that we so badly needed. The envelope was from Gwen, one of our loving church sisters. We prayed and thank God for always showing up when we need Him most. There are other similar stories that have helped to anchor our faith and trust in the loving and caring God that we serve.

"But my God shall supply all your need according to his riches in glory by Christ Jesus" (Phil. 4:19).

Chapter Twenty-Two

Saved from Suicide by Free at Last

This story is an inspiring account from a book written by one of my fellow literature evangelists, Bea Johnson Padron.

Hazel answered the door with fear, and I needed to gain her friendship within minutes. She was almost blind with hereditary cataracts. She bought the book, *Free at Last*, even though there was no one to read it to her. Every Monday morning, I would drive about thirty-five miles to her house to be there by 9 a.m. I would then spend an hour reading and discussing the book with her. Later, she moved to Virginia and met a literature evangelist there who knew me. While talking with this literature evangelist, Hazel revealed that that time when I came to her door, she was planning to take her own life. Hazel told the literature evangelist that because I came, read, and prayed with her, she felt encouraged, and her faith in God increased. Hazel never said anything to me about wanting to take her life, and I was surprised to learn that God used me in that way to help her.

There are times when people are crying out to God for help, and God will use us to answer their prayers. This is what happened with the Israelites in Egypt when they cried out to God because of their oppression. God called Moses to go and deliver His people. When we hear the cry of the lost, as God hears their cries, we will gladly say, "Lord, here am I, send me." (Padron, *Experiences of God's Power with Three Hours to Live*, pp. 96, 97)

Chapter Twenty-Three

FAQ at the Door

One summer evening in the early 1980s, I was canvassing in an area not far from the Philadelphia Zoo. Accompanying me that evening was Miss Cynthia Forbes, a wonderful Christian young woman who is now my beautiful wife. She came along that evening to get a firsthand experience on how I do the literature work that she heard me talk about so often.

As we started knocking on doors, we noticed that further down the street there was a home that had a good number of people sitting on the porch. The folks were laughing and enjoying their conversation. Seeing them, I said to myself that perhaps when I get to that porch, I might be able make a group presentation.

The Hope of a Group Presentation

As we got closer to the house, I noticed that people began leaving little by little until finally when I reached to the gate only two people were sitting on the porch, which were the couple who lived there. So, I knocked on the gate.

"May I help you?' they said in a somewhat unwelcoming voice. I introduced myself. "Good evening, I am Mr. Roberts from the Family Health Education Service. My partner is Miss Cynthia Forbes. We are sharing information in your community about health. You wouldn't mind us speaking to you for just a few moments, would you?"

Reluctantly, they consented and invited us on their porch. I was impressed to show them the medical books, and while talking to them about it, they warmed up to us. While I was writing up the contract, the husband told us that when they saw us coming down their street, they thought we were those Seventh-day Adventists. His wife corrected him immediately, telling him that he was mistaken and that they had thought we were Jehovah's Witnesses. He insisted that he was not mistaken; he thought we were Seventh-day Adventists. As they argued among themselves, I restrained myself from being embroiled in their dispute and remained silent while writing up the contract.

The husband was very interested in the medical books. He wanted to learn more on how to take better care of own personal health. His wife also related that he was previously in the hospital for heart issues, and she was very happy about the section of the book that showed how to eat healthy. She felt that would be of great benefit to him.

Finally, he gave me a $60 down payment on the medical set and asked me to bring it with me on my next visit. We thanked them for their hospitality as we made our way to the next door.

What I learned from that experience is that Jesus should be our example in all things. There are times when silence is the prudent thing to do.

"And when he was accused of the chief priests and elders, he answered nothing. Then said Pilate unto him, Hearest thou not how many things they witness against thee? And he answered him to never a word; insomuch that the governor marvelled greatly" (Matt. 27:12–14).

Mistaken Identity

What I also learned from our last customer is that there are many times when innocent people doing a good work can be easily mistaken for someone else.

As a Christian literature salesman, I was never surprised that I would be met with objections. Some people object to avoid an interview and do not want to be bothered. There are some people who object to avoid purchasing, while others object just to avoid making immediate decisions. Another objection is the one made because of a prejudicial or preconceived notion of who I am. The husband and wife who I sold the medical books to are a good example. It was not until they saw the nature of my work that they warmed up to me and made a purchase that was to their benefit.

There were times when people asked what denomination puts out the books that I was selling. I had to explain that the real objective of my work was to help people, whoever they are, whatever their religious affiliation, learn how to live healthy lives and also to encourage people to have a more abundant spiritual life as well. There were other times when people asked me about my personal religious affiliation. Even though I always avoided directly getting into a discussion on religion, there were times when it was inevitable, and I had to explain why and what I believed.

That is why the apostle encourages us this way, "But sanctify the Lord God in your hearts: and be ready always to give an answer to every man that asketh you a reason of the hope that is in you with meekness and fear" (1 Peter 3:15).

Questions People Generally Asked

Many times, people ask sincere questions in order to determine whether to buy or not to buy what you are selling. For example, some people ask if they are Jehovah's Witness books. Others ask if the books have anything to do with Baptists, Catholics, Seventh-day Adventists, or Methodist publications. These are genuine concerns, and people have the right to know what they are buying.

Jesus had a balanced ministry. He did not just spend His time in preaching and teaching, but He also spent a great portion of His time healing the maladies of people with great compassion. Everybody wants to have better health regardless of religion. So, the medical books on health and nutrition have been the medium through which many who were suffering in declining health have been restored to more abundant living.

However, as I stated earlier, there were other times when people asked me about my religious affiliation, and even though I tried very hard to avoid getting into discussion on religion, there were times when it was inevitable to avoid it, and I had to explain why and what I believed. As a result, based on my explanations, many people request Bible studies, and after studying the Bible, they make decisions on their own volitions and convictions on what to do.

Below are some of the honest questions that people generally asked and the answers that I provided based on the Bible and the Bible alone.

Q. What is the meaning of the name Seventh-day Adventist?

A. Seventh-day, referred to Saturday, the seventh day of the week, which I observe as the Lord's Sabbath, according to the Ten Commandments in Exodus 20:8–11.

An Adventist is a person who believe in the imminent second coming of Christ. So, when you put the two words together, Seventh-day and

Adventist, it describes a person who observes the seventh-day Sabbath and is also looking forward to the second coming of Jesus.

Q. Why do you keep Saturday while the vast majority of Christians keep Sunday?

A. My personal reason for keeping the Sabbath holy is because Jesus kept it, and I am following in His steps.

Q. But Mr. Roberts, wasn't the Sabbath for the Jews, Sunday for Christians, and Friday for the Muslims?

A. I can only follow what the Bible says. "And he said unto them, The sabbath was made for man, and not man for the sabbath: Therefore, the Son of man is Lord also of the sabbath" (Mark 2:27, 28). Jesus said it was made for all of humanity.

Q. But Mr. Roberts, why are you placing so much significance on that day?

A. Actually, I don't, but God places greater significance than I do.

> If thou turn away thy foot from the sabbath, from doing thy pleasure on my holy day; and call the sabbath a delight, the holy of the LORD, honourable; and shalt honour him, not doing thine own ways, nor finding thine own pleasure, nor speaking thine own words: Then shalt thou delight thyself in the LORD; and I will cause thee to ride upon the high places of the earth, and feed thee with the heritage of Jacob thy father: for the mouth of the LORD hath spoken it. (Isa. 58:13, 14)

Q. Come on Mr. Roberts, that was the Old Testament. Did the New Testament believers practice that?

A. "And Paul, as his manner was, went in unto them, and three sabbath days reasoned with them out of the scriptures" (Acts 17:2).

"And when the Jews were gone out of the synagogue, the Gentiles besought that these words might be preached to them the next sabbath" (Acts 13:42).

"And he reasoned in the synagogue every sabbath, and persuaded the Jews and the Greeks.... And he continued there a year and six months, teaching the word of God among them" (Acts 18:4, 11).

Q. Then why did it say this in Colossians 2:16, "Let no man therefore judge you in meat, or in drink, or in respect of an holyday, or of the new moon, or of the sabbath days"?

A. I agree with you on this scripture because I don't observe Passover or the Day of Atonement, which was a yearly sabbath of rest, or any of the other feast days that pointed to the work of the anticipated Messiah. Christ came, lived, died, and fulfilled them. However, according to Isaiah, God will still reserve the weekly Sabbath as a day of worship in the new earth where I plan to be.

> For as the new heavens and the new earth, which I will make, shall remain before me, saith the LORD, so shall your seed and your name remain. And it shall come to pass, that from one new moon to another, and from one sabbath to another, shall all flesh come to worship before me, saith the LORD. (Isa. 66:22, 23)

During the course of literature evangelism, I have met people across the spectrum of religion. I never entered into needless debates, but I used the Scriptures and the Scriptures alone and did as Jesus did when He was challenged. "But he answered and said, It is written, Man shall not live by bread alone, but by every word that proceedeth out of the mouth of God" (Matt. 4:4). It is always wise to exalt the name of Jesus because He is our example in all things. "And I, if I be lifted up from the earth, will draw all men unto me" (John 12:32).

In consultation with their pastor, someone gave me a Bible passage to read with a note that indicated why we are not obligated to keep the Sabbath today. The passage was taken from Numbers 15:32, 35, which says, "And while the children of Israel were in the wilderness, they found a man that gathered sticks upon the sabbath day. And the LORD said unto Moses, The man shall be surely put to death: all the congregation shall stone him with stones without the camp."

This verse was given to me to prove that because people are not being stoned to death today for breaking the Sabbath, it is done away with and Christians are no longer under any obligation to keep it. It sounds like a very good argument, and to many, that is all it takes to convince them. However, we cannot ignore the importance of other passages of Scripture.

What About Adultery?

In Leviticus 20:10, it states, "And the man that committeth adultery with another man's wife, even he that committeth adultery with his neighbour's wife, the adulterer and the adulteress shall surely be put to death." So, here we have the seventh commandment, which says if one commits adultery, they should be put to death. Does that mean that because no one is put to death today in our churches as a result of committing adultery that adultery is no longer a sin? Absolutely not!

So, why not apply the same measuring stick to the fourth commandment, which reminds us to keep the Sabbath? Is it no longer in force just because people are not being put to death for breaking it today? The Bible should be our only safeguard when we come to difficult questions. To adequately answer this question, in regards to the sin of adultery and the sin of Sabbath breaking, the apostle Peter says this, "The Lord knoweth how to deliver the godly out of temptations, and to reserve the unjust unto the day of judgment to be punished" (2 Peter 2:9). The big question is whose Sabbath shall we obey? God-made or man-made?

Man-Made Sabbath—On Keeping Sunday Holy

Fifth Recommendation: Do not shop or work on Sunday, if you can possibly avoid it. From all that has been written, it is clear that, for the Christian, buying and selling on the Sabbath is abhorrent and irreligious.

The Founding Fathers and pioneer politicians of all the original colonies had strict laws requiring church attendance and banning work, travel, sports and commerce on Sunday. In the 17th Century such regulations were written on blue paper, and they were still referred to as "blue laws." The courts in the United States, and recently the Supreme Court, have ruled on the necessity of one legal day of rest a week, and so have established the Sabbath as one of the civil institutions of the States.

Since the 1950s there has been constant pressure to repeal or relax these laws. As the courts and labor unions have pointed out, a day of rest is important. For the genuine Christian, however, there is no "business as usual" on Sunday, primarily because of religious reasons. The Catholic who buys or sells works unnecessarily on Sunday is destroying the sanctity of this day and is giving the worst of example. As Pope John wrote: "It is with great sorrow that we note and deplore the ever-increasing neglect of, if not downright disrespect for this sacred law." (Whealon, S.T.L., S.S.L., D.D., *Living the Catholic Faith Today*, p. 69)

God-Made Sabbath—On Keeping the Seventh Day Holy

"If thou turn away thy foot from the sabbath, from doing thy pleasure on my holy day; and call the sabbath a delight, the holy of the LORD, honourable; and shalt honour him, not doing thine own ways, nor finding thine own pleasure, nor speaking thine own words" (Isa. 58:13).

> Remember the sabbath day, to keep it holy. Six days shalt thou labour, and do all thy work: But the seventh day is the sabbath of the LORD thy God: in it thou shalt not do any work, thou, nor thy son, nor thy daughter, thy manservant, nor thy maidservant, nor thy cattle, nor thy stranger that is within thy gates: For in six days the LORD made heaven and earth, the sea, and all that in them is, and rested the seventh day: wherefore the LORD blessed the sabbath day, and hallowed it. (Exod. 20:8–11)

After I give an answer from the Holy Scriptures, my work is dome. I leave the rest to the Holy Spirit and the person to exercise their liberty of their conscience and their freedom of choice.

Chapter Twenty-Four

The Fifth Miracle at the Door

The Door That Changed My Life Forever

I was 23 years old when I became a literature evangelist in 1976, and I was one of the youngest in my area. At that time, I was a full-time employee at a medical institution, but I was determined to join the band of literature evangelists as a part-time worker.

I was also very actively involved doing missionary work in my church, so literature work became my main focus of evangelism. Shortly after I began, the church took notice that many new converts were being added to the church as a result of my work. These new converts consisted of not just adults, but young men, young women, children, and even entire families at times.

Why Is He Still Single?

During this same time, people also began to notice that I remained single in spite of the available young women in the church. What they were not aware of was that I had made a covenant with God in regards to my future, which included the acquisition of a house and to find a virtuous Christian wife. In making this covenant, I took a sheet of paper and divided it in three categories under which I wrote down what I desired of the Lord.

My Spiritual Goals

The first category was entitled, "My Spiritual Goals." There, I wrote down all my spiritual needs and my desire to walk perfectly with the Lord. I included many of my favorite Bible promises, such as, "But seek ye first the kingdom of God, and his righteousness; and all these things shall be added unto you" (Matt. 6:33). I wanted to be holy.

My Physical Goals

The second category was entitled, "My Physical Goals." In this category, I pledged to present my body as a living sacrifice to God by caring for it in obedience to the healthful living principles given to us in the Bible. I claimed the promises of God where He wished that I would prosper and be in health as my soul prospers. And I asked Him to keep me healthy, happy, and holy. "Beloved, I wish above all things that thou mayest prosper and be in health, even as thy soul prospereth" (3 John 2). I wanted to be healthy.

My Temporal Goals

The third category was "My Temporal Goals." One of the first temporal goals I had was my desire to acquire a home. I told the Lord that I was not going to search for one, fearing that I might make the wrong choice. So, I asked the Lord to let someone tell me of an available house, even if I didn't ask them to look or search for me. That would be the sign of the answer to my request.

The second temporal goal on the list was for the Lord to find me a virtuous wife. I also told the Lord that I was not going to search for a wife, but if He had one prepared for me, He would have to reveal it to me at the appropriate time. So, by faith, I described to Him several things that I personally desired about that wife. This included, among other things, preference in nationality, but not exclusively. But of all the things I desired to see, most importantly, were her character traits. I needed to see humility, meekness, unselfishness, a Christlike character, and genuine love for God and for me. "Whoso findeth a wife findeth a good thing, and obtaineth favour of the LORD" (Prov. 18:22). I wanted to be happy.

God's Providence

In 1978, by divine providence, I met Leonie, a lady whose Caribbean accent caught my attention while she was talking on a public phone.

I introduced myself to her and learned that we were from the same country. After a brief and friendly conversation, we exchanged telephone numbers and parted. Subsequently, neither of us made contact with each other until a year later.

One Year Later

As it turned out, like a rerun, I saw the same lady speaking on the same public telephone one year later. She explained how she had misplaced my number and didn't have any way of contacting me. So, once again, we exchanged numbers. This time she extended an invitation for me to come and meet her family whenever I am in her area.

The Day I Met Her Family

On a Sunday morning in July of 1979, it so happened that I was going to look at a car not far from Leonie's neighborhood, so I called her to ask if it would be convenient for me to stop by her home. She was glad to hear from me and confirmed that I could stop by.

In the meantime, before I arrived, she told her family about me and how we had met. In fact, I later learned that the family was expecting me to be a tall handsome man and not a short unassuming person like me.

When I arrived at her house, Leonie's daughter, Deanna, answered the door. Leonie introduced me to Joyce, her older sister, and her three daughters, one of whom was Cynthia. They were very kind and friendly people, and they made me feel very welcomed in their home. My visit was short, but before I left, I extended an invitation to Deanna and Cynthia to visit my church.

God Fulfilled the Covenant

I never imagined in my wildest dreams that knocking on the door of 5453 Regent Street in July of 1979 would be the turning point in changing my life forever. Only God in His omniscience knew that it would culminate in the answer to my covenant goal for a wife as well as the answer to Cynthia's prayer for a husband.

When Cynthia first saw me during that short visit, it made a profound and positive impression on her mind. She later told me that before I left her home that day, she went upstairs to her room and made a prophetic utterance to herself, stating that God had sent her the husband for whom she had been praying. That was her faith at work, and she left it at that, not knowing how, when, or what God was going to do.

Bible Study

The following Sabbath, Deanna and Cynthia paid a visit to my church. I was very glad to see them. At the service, they were introduced as my visitors and following the service, I drove them to their home. Before I left, I asked them if they would like to take Bible studies, and Deanna gladly accepted the offer and consented to start the study the following Friday evening.

Cynthia, on the other hand, was already studying with the Jehovah Witnesses and attending their Kingdom Hall, so she was not interested in getting involved with another Bible study.

Cynthia Joined the Study

Even though Cynthia was not an active participant in the study, she would sit in and listen, and as a result, she became intrigued with the new way of studying the Bible. She was gaining a greater understanding of the amazing Bible prophecies of Daniel and the Revelation and the soon coming of Christ. She developed an unquenchable thirst in her desire to learn more and more until she became fully committed to the studies.

Cynthia Discontinued Studying with the Jehovah Witnesses

After Cynthia fully committed herself to her new studies, she met with her former instructors from the Kingdom Hall and informed them of her decision. They told her that she could not serve two masters, so they would discontinue their studies with her.

Is She the One?

As the studies progressed, I asked a Bible worker, Roberta, to take over the studies. Eventually, Deanna lost interest and dropped out of the study, leaving Cynthia as the sole one continuing with the study. In an effort to learn more, Cynthia began to visit the church on a regular basis until it became permanent.

At my church, the members began to wonder if Cynthia was the one that I would finally choose to be my wife. But the fact of the matter was that Cynthia and I had not developed mutual friendship in that direction. Prior to me meeting Cynthia, I was in a friendship-relationship with Adnor, another lovely, young, Christian woman from the North Philadelphia Seventh-day Adventist Church where I once attended. Adnor and I both cared about each other and had a great relationship. She also loved the literature work and became a part of the team for a short while. During that time, many of my fellow literature evangelists began to wonder what I was waiting for and began asking me when was I planning to tie the knot with Adnor. But God was working things out according to His divine purpose, and I had no clue.

While attending a weekend seminar at my church, I gained some valuable insight from a Christian psychologist. According to the psychologist, there are three secrets that married people don't tell single people. He emphasized that the vast majority of people who get divorced are still in love with each other.

He said that there are seven important things in making a marriage happy, and in the order of importance, love is down at number six. He continued to say that there are five things that are more important than love in making a marriage work, and if those five things are not there, then love makes no difference in the relationship.

The first secret was not love but rather how many things we have in common. That is the reason why the Bible asks the question, "Can two walk together, except they agreed?" (Amos 3:3).

At that time in my life, I knew within myself that I was not ready for marriage. Adnor and I were very honest with each other, and after talking about our relationship and the future, we came to a mutual and amicable conclusion that it would be prudent for both of us to move on with our lives rather than to get married and not be ready for it.

The discussion we had did not mar the Christian friendship that we shared, but it was an incentive to faithfully follow where God led. For me, it was a very difficult decision to make, but we could not allow our feelings to dictate our future. We had to follow the Spirit's leading.

A Prophetic Dream of Confirmation

Around the same time that Adnor and I made our mutual decision, Sister Bea Johnson had a prophetic dream in which she saw Adnor walking down to the church altar to be married to someone else other than me. Frantically, Sister Johnson cried out in her dream, "No, no, it's supposed to be Brother Roberts!" After she described her dream to me, I assured her that the dream was true and that God was preparing her and the other literature evangelists in the group to accept that reality to be God's will.

Meanwhile, at the church, some of the available young ladies with whom I was very friendly honestly hoped that I would become more than just casual friend. I have learned that, as a young man, one must be very careful of not being overly friendly with the opposite sex. Often times, it may inadvertently send the wrong signal that would cause hurt and disappointment. Thankfully, in my case, whatever misunderstandings and differences existed, they were reconciled in the spirit of Christian love and forgiveness.

At the same time, Cynthia was growing in her relationship with Christ and decided that she wanted to be baptized. In March of 1980, she finally was baptized and became a full-fledged member of the church. One Saturday night in that same year, the church went hay riding on a social venture. When I picked up Cynthia and got to the church to join with the others, the bus had already left, and because I did not have the address of the location, we stayed behind.

An Honest Conversation

While we sat in the car, I timidly began to share with Cynthia how I felt about her. I told her how when she was not at church that I missed her dearly. I also told her how much I admired the gentle way she treated the elderly and how she showed love and compassion towards the little children. I reminded her that the first date that we had together other than being at church was when she accompanied me to a funeral service. I told her that her willingness to join me impressed me and showed me her meekness and humility, which I deeply admired. I finally admitted that my admiration and affection for her was growing strong.

On her part, Cynthia admitted that the feeling was mutual in all respects. For the first time, we held hands together as a sign of our mutual confirmation. That night was the beginning of a pure, honest, loving, and committed Christian relationship. Naturally, as a result of our commitment, people began to take notice, and as was with the case of Adnor, they began to ask questions as to when I was going to tie the knot with Cynthia.

An Answer to the First Request

In November of 1982, God answered my request for the acquisition of a house. If you recall, I told the Lord that I was not going to look for a house or ask anyone to look for one. I specifically asked Him to find it for me and let me know when it is ready. Accordingly, I received a phone call from my beloved mother. She stated that there was a lovely house available, and all I needed to do was to move in.

I took that as a sign that the Lord was speaking to me and acted promptly. The miracle was that even though I did not have all the funds, God provided, and in a couple weeks, I was the proud owner of a beautiful house according to my covenant with the Lord. "Ask, and it shall be given you; seek, and ye shall find; knock, and it shall be opened unto you" (Matt. 7:7).

The Night She Became the Jewel in My Crown

As the sun set on Saturday evening, November 19, 1983, two years after Cynthia and I had pledge ourselves to a mutual, honest, Christian relationship, she became the jewel in my crown. We were joined together in holy matrimony at the Havertown Seventh-day Adventist Church. The ceremony was officiated by Pastor William Linthicum, assisted by the late Elder James Warren, Jr.

We started a wonderful, loving life together as husband and wife, and our union was blessed with two adorable children. Our daughter, Khalilah, born in June of 1985 and our son, Daniel, born in January of 1987.

The Second Request Answered

In retrospect, God answered the prayer request in my covenant list in the exact order and priority as I had placed them. A house first and then a virtuous wife to complete that house into a blessed home.

"Who can find a virtuous woman? for her price is far above rubies. The heart of her husband doth safely trust in her, so that he shall have no need of spoil. She will do him good and not evil all the days of her life" (Prov. 31:10–12).

"And in that day ye shall ask me nothing. Verily, verily, I say unto you, Whatsoever ye shall ask the Father in my name, he will give it you" (John 16:23).

This love experience between Cynthia and I has truly been a miracle at the door. Who would have thought that by speaking to a complete stranger on a public phone that it would eventually lead to finding the love of my life and my lifelong partner? Only by the grace of God.

My Covenant Between Me and My God

Date_____

My pledge: (Gen 28:18–22)

A. To live a consistent, committed Christian life

B. To be faithful in tithes and offerings

C. To share the message of God's love and truth with others

_____

My Spiritual Goals: God's promise (Matt 5:6)

A. To be filled with the Holy Spirit

B. To have daily devotion and prayer

C. To be ready for the glorious return of Jesus

My Physical Goals: God's promise (Exod. 15:26)

A. To live a healthy lifestyle

B. To practice the eight laws of health, which includes sunshine, fresh open air, daily exercise, trust in God, proper rest, adequate water intake, temperance, and proper nutrition.

C. To be happy, healthy, and holy

My Temporal Goals: God's promise (Phil. 4:19)

A. To acquire a home

B. To find a virtuous wife and have a happy home

C. To have blessed children

When I shared this this covenant plan idea with my church, the Southwest Philadelphia Adventist Church, many tried it, and it was a wonderful blessing for them. Every New Year's Eve, instead of making resolutions, they did the covenant plan. They would put it in an envelope, address to their heavenly Father, and pray over it. During the year, they highlighted the requests that were answered. It's a miracle when you write things down.

Why not try it and prove the Lord and see if He will "open you the windows of heaven, and pour you out a blessing, that there shall not be room enough to receive it" (Mal. 3:10).

Chapter Twenty-Five

The Sixth Miracle at the Door

When adversity knocked at my door, it left my two children in a coma.

How could this be? Two young siblings in a coma, simultaneously? That's unimaginable! That was the big question that faced the doctors at the Children's Hospital of Philadelphia in 1988.

Thus far, throughout this book, you have journeyed with me from door to door and entered many homes. You have experienced miracles in changed lives, success stories, dangerous encounters, and even laughter. But what about my door? Who was it that came knocking at my door? Like Job, it was not a person, but instead, it was adversity that came knocking at my door, and it entered without an invitation. Please join me and my wife, and learn about the devastating crucibles that literally turned our world upside down and how we overcame.

It All Started with Fever

On Sunday afternoon, February 24, 1991, Khalilah, my five-year-old daughter, began shivering from a fever. Like most parents, we gave her Tylenol and observed her carefully. However, for Cynthia and me, our concern increased whenever our children developed a fever. This attitude was not an overreaction but stemmed from a horrifying experience, which had almost taken the lives of both of our children three years earlier in 1988.

Four Years Earlier

It began in 1988 when our son, Daniel, just thirteen months old, and our daughter, Khalilah, almost three years old, simultaneously developed a fever. We gave them Tylenol as we normally did at all other times and hoped the fever would subside. The fever continued the following day. We noticed that they were getting very lethargic, sleepy, and would not respond to us as usual. We felt that this was grossly abnormal, so we immediately rushed them to the children's hospital. Recognizing that their condition was very serious, the doctors admitted them.

By that time, both children were comatose. The doctors, nurses, and technicians began running various tests to determine the cause of their illness. I remembered them pumping charcoal in both of their stomachs in case they had ingested poison.

In the meantime, my wife and I were questioned relentlessly as to the what, when, where, and how all this could possibly have happened to both children. Well, after all the test results were evaluated and all of the possible causes ruled out, the spinal fluid test results revealed that they had contracted viral encephalitis. How that happened, we do not know. Some suggested that it may have been reaction from their vaccine, but who was to tell.

In just one short afternoon, both our lives were instantly changed from normalcy to an inexpressible nightmare. Our lives were being turned upside down. But thankfully, with the superb care of the wonderful nurses and doctors and the fervent prayers of family, friends, and church members, our son awoke from his coma in just about seven days and was discharged from the hospital one week later. Our daughter, on the other hand, remained in her comatose condition for almost a month after.

The Damage Sustained

When she finally awoke, we discovered that she had not only incurred physical and neurological damage, but she had also totally lost her vision. This heart-wrenching reality took us to another unbelievable level of stress and unimaginable worry.

Our daughter's attitude through all of that trauma amazed us. While we were crying, confused, and baffled, she, on the other hand, was carefree, composed, and happy. Although she could not physically see, she showed no sign of alarm, worry, or concern. As long as she knew that we were there, felt our love, the warmth of our hugs, kisses, and heard the cheerful sound of her little brother's recorded voice, she was happy as she ever could be. Her love, confidence, and security in us was enough to let her feel that she would be alright soon.

That's the reason she woke up early every morning singing the chorus, "Happy, happy, happy, happy in the Lord! Keeping His commandments and trusting in His Word! I want you to know God's promises are true, and that's why I am happy, happy in the Lord!" She would sing that as well as many other choruses. She had learned them during our morning and evening family worship time at home. My wife and I were very happy that in our daughter's time of trouble, her childish faith was not anchored in fairy tales' songs but on songs that kept her little heart trusting in God. Her jovial spirit and melodious voice brought much joy to her hospital rehab unit and continued until she was discharged. Khalilah was well-remembered because of the joy she shared in spite of her crucibles.

Lots of Therapy

After much physical and occupational therapy, she regained her physical mobility, but she had not recovered her loss of sight. While Cynthia stayed home to take care of our son, Daniel, I spent most of my time at the hospital with Khalilah. On Sabbaths, I would wheel her to the chapel where I would tell her Bible stories, sing, and pray together.

The Sabbath Miracle

One Sabbath morning after she and I had prayed together, I was sitting beside her hospital bed with my hand resting beside her. Then out of nowhere, she said something that startled me. In a tiny little whisper, I heard her softly say, "That's your watch, Daddy."

Dumbfounded and baffled, I asked, "What did you say, Khalilah?" Again, she repeated it and pointed to the watch on my arm. It was miraculous! I realized she had regained her sight, and my heart was overwhelmed with ineffable joy.

I was so elated; I jumped into action and got her in the wheelchair to race to the chapel. As we approached the door to exit the unit, she pointed to the huge picture on the door and uttered, "That's Mickey Mouse." That was the greatest confirmation that she could see again. Now she could in reality say, "I was once blind, but now I am able to see again" (see John 9:25).

Khalilah soon recovered her full vision but was left with some residual physical and mental challenges for which she required special education. Her brother did not suffer as severely as she did. He was visually impaired and suffered with seizures for a while. However, he was eventually taken off seizure medication and never had to take it again.

Because of Daniel's and Khalilah's amazing recovery from that episode of illness in 1988, some people referred to them as miracle children. On the other hand, these were very difficult and trying times for Cynthia and me. As a newly married couple, our lives were suddenly fraught with great physical and emotional stress, along with enormous new challenges. Worst of all was the enormous financial obligations that we incurred. It added to our burden and made it seemed that our challenges were insurmountable.

The Second Round

Now that you know what happened in 1988, I have no doubt that you can understand what I meant earlier about the concern that Cynthia and I had when our daughter began shivering with a fever in 1991. Like a rerun, her fever would not subside. That Wednesday afternoon, I took her to the clinic at Thomas Jefferson University Hospital. After the doctor examined her, he said that her fever seemed to stem from a virus. He instructed me to take her home, continue to give her Tylenol for the fever, and if she did not get any better, I should bring her back to the clinic.

We traveled home on public transportation from the clinic. Khalilah slept on my lap all the way. When we got off the transportation, I noticed that her walking was much slower than usual, and she was missing her steps. By the time we entered our house, she wanted to go to bed and did not care to eat or drink.

The following day, I reluctantly went to work while my wife stayed home with her. It was very difficult for me to function well at work. The concern of my sick child dominated my thoughts. I could not help calling home repeatedly to check on her condition. At about 1:00 p.m. when I called home again, there was no answer. This caused all manner of thoughts to flash through my mind. I instinctively ran to the chapel and prayed and cried, then returned to my work area. By the time I returned, my wife had called to notify me that our daughter was just admitted to the hospital. She was weeping on the phone as she tried to explain that our daughter wouldn't wake up. "She just won't wake up," she exclaimed.

I immediately left work and headed for the hospital. I ran, I cried, and I prayed all the way to my daughter's side.

In the Intensive Care

Well, there she was, lying in the intensive care unit at Thomas Jefferson University Hospital in a coma again. We hovered over her as a hen would her little chicks. Her eyes were closed, and there was no motion except the rise and fall of her chest from her breathing. She was totally oblivious to our touch, our kisses, and our moist tears that fell on her cheeks. It all felt as if it were a dream, but it was not. The attending pediatrician immediately had her placed on a respirator for her safety, fearing that her breathing could stop because of her condition.

After a thorough workup through blood tests, a brain scan, etc. it was determined that she had a brain stem lesion. The lesion was causing swelling in the brain stem and immediate surgery was recommended. We were overwhelmed with the sudden unknowns that we faced. This was the first time as a newly married couple that we were faced with such a crucial decision as to sign surgical consent forms that could affect our child's life for better or for worse. We wished that we could have unshackled ourselves from the doubts, the suspense, and the fears that controlled and tortured us.

Brain Surgery

While she was being prepared for surgery, there was an immediate call for a prayer vigil. Our families, friends, and fellow church members all responded. While in surgery, a group gathered in the waiting room and earnestly prayed for a favorable result. Those prayers, I must confess, were truly the resource that enabled us to maintain composure throughout the ordeal.

In the operating room, a craniotomy was being performed to obtain a biopsy from the lesion to determine if there was malignancy. After a couple of hours had passed, the doctor appeared and greeted us with a warm and pleasant smile that immediately dispelled our fears and anxiety. He reported to us that the result of the biopsy was benign. This wonderful news was music to our ears. Immediately, we felt liberated from a ton of pressure, and the gloom that had overshadowed us suddenly vanished.

Postoperatively, however, her recovery was complicated by meningitis, which created excess fluid build-up in her brain. The doctor told us that as a result of the excess fluid build-up, they would have to implant a device called an Ommaya Rickham reservoir. This was to be done in order to administer medications and also to retrieve cerebrospinal fluid. Her prognosis was uncertain and recovery was slow and tedious. It wasn't long before it became evident to us by her overall response that she had incurred significant physical and neurological damage, the extent of which could only be determined as time went on.

Taking Her Off the Ventilator

During her long recovery from surgery, the doctors were concerned because of her prolonged ventilator dependency. We were concerned as well and kept asking how long she would need to continue being on the ventilator. Each time that I asked the doctor, he would tell me that as soon as she showed a good gag response, they would attempt to remove the tracheal tube.

The Day She Almost Died

Of all the days during my daughter's stay in the hospital, Friday, March 22, 1991 was the most horrific one. My wife was home with our son, and I was with our daughter at the hospital. That morning, I do not know how much she was aware of my presence, but I laid my hand on her and prayed with her.

After that, her doctor checked her out and was quite surprised that she had a good gag. We were all praying for the day when they would remove the tracheal tube, and he was delighted as well. No one expected the nightmare that would follow the attempt to remove the tracheal tube. At first when they removed the tube, she seemed to be breathing fine on her own, but suddenly her oxygen saturation level and heart rate began to drop very rapidly.

They recognized that she was in trouble. It was truly a code blue, and they called for a rapid response. Trying to reintubate was difficult, and she was going into respiratory and cardiac arrest. They had to do resuscitation and apply electric shock to her heart, so they very quickly ushered me away from the scene to the waiting room. The only thing I could do was pray and pray because I was going through a horrifying emotional meltdown. I could not keep still because I could hear the commotions and observe the nurses and other personnel rushing back and forth while they all avoided looking in my direction, which, in itself, made me feel that the situation was very grave. The word death was flashing through my mind, and my thoughts became nebulous. Obviously, someone recognized my distress and quickly sent a social worker to stay with me and to try assuage my fears.

While I waited, I could feel a strange tremor going through my body. I thought that it was the end, and my daughter had not made it since it took so long for someone to reach out to me. But while I was cerebrating on it, there came the doctor walking towards me with a calm and optimistic look on his face. He put his hand on my shoulder with a sigh of relief. He said that we almost lost her, and it's a little setback, but thank God, she is stable. When I was able to pull myself together, I called my wife and tried to gently break the news to her of what had transpired. She was absolutely devastated and started to weep, but I did my best to console her.

We Need to Do a Tracheotomy

"Oh no, not a tracheotomy!" That was my response when the ENT doctor told us that they would have to perform a tracheotomy on my daughter as soon as possible. They explained that because she was on the ventilator for so long and also experienced the most recent trauma, she had developed tracheal stenosis, and it was necessary to do a tracheotomy for her to breathe on her own and give her airway time to heal from the stenosis.

On Monday, March 25, 1991, Khalilah had the tracheotomy done. She was looking great, and her breathing was excellent. During the period of her recovery, there was no specific treatment except antibiotics for the meningitis. Weeks had now passed, and we saw no signs of meaningful physical movements that indicated she was coming out of the coma, except sporadic opening and closing of her eyes.

In the meantime, no one wanted to give us false hope. When we inquired as to her prognosis, the doctors were somewhat reticent because they had no immediate answer that would allay our fears or give us some optimism. All they could say to us was, "Let's wait and see." In my heart, I understood how they felt. They would have loved to say to us that all would be well soon, but of course, they could not predict the future. We all had to wait it out.

The Use of Carrot Juice

During this waiting period, the doctor explained to us that our daughter had become anemic and would need a blood transfusion. The anemia, they explained, resulted from the amount of blood that had been drawn from her since she had been admitted, along with the obvious fact that she had not been able to eat. In response, my wife and I, along with her two sisters, Jenny and Lynn, immediately donated enough blood, so she would have it available if needed.

We were not comfortable with the thought of doing a blood transfusion, so if we had another available option, we would surely have welcomed it. What could we do to help replenish and build up her blood naturally and rapidly? We turned to the one thing that came to our mind that we thought could help. It was the use of raw organic carrot juice.

Several years earlier, I had read that information from a book about vegetable and fruit juices. "Raw carrot juice is a natural solvent for ulcerous and cancerous conditions" (Walker, *Fresh Vegetable and Fruit Juices*, p. 33).

Interestingly, on page 39 of the same book, it states that, "By means of the latest super-microscopes, it has been possible to determine that carrot juice molecule is exactly analogous to that of the blood molecule, a most interesting and revealing fact. No wonder we have found the juice of carrots so extremely beneficial."

After getting clearance from her doctor, my wife and I decided to feed it to her. So, on March 18, nineteen days after she was admitted, we started giving Khalilah carrot juice through her feeding tube. Twice daily, morning and evening, she received a pint of raw organic carrot juice. It became a part of her regular diet while she was there as a patient.

Amazingly, of all of the blood donated, she only required one of the units donated by my wife. After feeding her the carrot juice, her complexion became ruddy, and she was no longer anemic.

The Use of Red Clover Tea

During those long tedious weeks of waiting, Cynthia and I longed for some news of hope that would ease our anxiety and keep our optimism high, but there was none. Therefore, we turned to the use of herbs as an alternative to see if they would help to improve her condition and expedite her recovery.

Though I had been a vegetarian for more than twenty-five years, taking herbs had not been a part of my daily routine. It actually took my daughter's illness to rediscover the wonderful healing benefits of herbs and gain deeper knowledge in the science of natural healing.

I learned that herbs are actually food. They are loaded with nutrients such as vitamins, minerals, and enzymes that the body uses to maintain health. When we eat these nourishing herbs, they provide the raw material that the body in turn uses to do its own healing work. It's that simple.

The first herb that we thought of giving to our daughter during her hospitalization was red clover. It was introduced to me by an herbalist that a friend had recommended. We listened to his experiences in helping others and also read a book on how red clover in combination with other herbs helped a man to eradicate his brain tumor. That information sealed our decision to try it.

On April 2, two months into her stay in the hospital, my wife and I had a conference with a group of doctors, social workers, and other health care professionals to discuss the future care of our child. They explained to us that our daughter's outcome was uncertain, and that they did not have a definite explanation for her condition. Even the results of a muscle biopsy that they thought might yield some clues as to the how, what, and why of her condition was inconclusive. With that, they recommended trying her on a special vitamin therapy that might help. A side effect, however, could be some allergic reaction or low blood sugar. Before they could start her on it, we, as the parents, would need to sign a consent form to give them authorization. They told us to take some time and think it over.

While we had everyone sitting at the conference table, we took the opportunity to explain the idea we had of giving herbs to her that we felt could help in her recovery. We explained that since herbs are considered food and not drugs, and since she was not on any medications that could cause an adverse reaction, we felt that she should not be deprived of them. They said they had no objections. That same evening, we started feeding her the red clover tea through her feeding tube. Now she was having not only carrot juice but also red clover tea twice daily.

> Red Clover is one of God's greatest blessings to man. Very pleasant to take, and a wonderful blood purifier. Combined with equal parts of Blue Violet, Burdock, Yellow dock, dandelion root, rock rose and Golden Seal, it is a most powerful remedy for cancerous growths and leprosy affections, also pellagra. (Kloss, *The Original Back to Eden*, p. 301)

Applying Herbs to the Soles of the Feet

After we got my daughter started on the red clover tea, I contacted a well-known herbalist from California to ascertain additional information that could be helpful in her condition. He was quite adept in the field of natural healing and imparted some invaluable information to me, including some herbs that he said could help to melt her lesion. Through his knowledge, I gained greater insight in other ways of administering herbs to a person when they are too sick to take it orally.

After doing some research on the nutritional values and traditional uses of the herbs that were suggested, I purchased them in powdered form from an herbal company and combined them into one mix in order to make a poultice. To make the poultice, I took some of the powder and put it into a small jar then added some aloe vera gel and some slippery elm powder. I kept the jar tightly closed so that the paste would remain moist.

Each night, we applied the paste to the soles of her feet. The next thing we did was quite important. We covered her feet with plastic. This was done to keep the herbs moist during the night. After the herbs were applied came the wonderful miracle of the body's ability to absorb the properties of the herbs via the soles of the feet and use them to do its own healing.

I was truly convinced that the immediate improvements that Cynthia and I saw after starting Khalilah on the herbs were a direct result of their use. There was nothing else to attribute it to, except that one could say "time heals."

Because of this, the word got around the unit that the little girl in the ICU was being fed with herbal tea and carrot juice. This, of course, sparked some curiosity. So much so that quite a number of the employees began asking us questions about herbs.

One of the nurses, greatly concerned about her sick father, asked me what herbs I would suggest for him. Of course, I was not as knowledgeable then to give valuable suggestions as I am now. One of the doctors, who felt impressed about the red clover herb, also inquired on how he could obtain information on it. I gladly gave him the only copy of the book I had. The specific combination of herbs that I used on the sole of Khalilah's feet was as follows: golden seal, mullein, lobelia, echinacea, catnip, and parsley. These were mixed into a poultice with aloe vera gel and slippery elm powder.

After my daughter awoke from her coma, she was discharged from the hospital on April 15 and transferred to a children's rehabilitation hospital where she would remain a patient for seven long months until her discharge on November 13, 1991.

Unimaginable Blessing

God would have it that Thomas Jefferson University Hospital acquired and absorbed the children's rehabilitation hospital at the same location where I worked. It made life so much easier for Cynthia to look after our son at home while I could see our daughter every day during work. God had surely given me an adorable wife that was and is second to none. Throughout all these trials, I realized He certainly answered my prayer from the covenant that I made with Him back in 1979. She has been the most precious jewel in my crown.

Herbs for Her Incontinence

During Khalilah's recovery at rehab, it became evident that she had a serious case of incontinence. She was not able to control or sense the need to urinate. It was recommended that we consult a urologist to diagnose the extent of her condition. After a urodynamic test was done to assess her bladder function, the doctor's diagnosis was that she had a neurogenic bladder, resulting from her brain stem and meningitis complication. He recommended a drug therapy first to treat her condition, but if that did not help her, the only other option to consider, was some type of surgical procedure.

After he explained the two options, I asked him about the side effects of the drugs that were recommended. I also asked him if there would be a problem using some natural herbs first to see if they would help her condition before starting her on the recommended drug therapy. He assured us that as the parents, we had the right to do so.

Shortly after that go ahead, I had a conference with the primary physician regarding the use of herbs to help my daughter's bladder problem. He was very impressed with what we presented and gladly consented. He told us to bring the herb in, so he could write the orders in her chart and have the nurses administer it with her meals according to the recommendation on the bottle.

The name of the herbal combination was called URY (urinary maintenance), a product we obtained from a reputable herbal company. Amazingly, in a relatively short time of about seven days after taking this herbal combination, Khalilah's condition improved so significantly that she was able to tell the nurses that she had the urge to urinate. It was amazing to us how in such a short period of time, her body responded so positively to the herbs with such fantastic results. Since the summer of 1991 to the present moment that I am writing, she still maintains full control of her bladder function.

The specific herbs contained in that combination were as follows: vitamins A (beta-carotene), C, and E, zinc, selenium, barley grass, asparagus stem, astragalus root, broccoli flowers, cabbage leaf, reishi mushroom, parthenium aerial parts and root, pau d'arco inner bark, schisandra fruit, eleuthero root, wheat grass, and myrrh gum.

Gotu Kola

Because of the tremendous trauma and assault on her brain, we were deeply concerned about her future mental health, especially her memory. We did some research to see what herb would be able to help her overall brain health. We finally settled on the herb gotu kola because it is said to help support memory function. After obtaining the herb, we started her on it immediately.

Anyone who know my daughter recognizes her enormous memory power. Often times when we cannot recall names, we would turn to her for help, and without fail, she is able to instantaneously recall the names we desire to know. She has the capacity to remember anyone that she has ever come in contact with or heard about. She is also a repository when it comes to the names of Bible characters.

As the Bible states in Psalm 104:14, "He causeth the grass to grow for the cattle, and herb for the service of man: that he may bring forth food out of the earth." By incorporating the brain and memory-boosting herb gotu kola in her daily life, God has richly blessed our daughter beyond measure.

Discharged From the Rehabilitation Hospital

After seven long months of extensive speech, occupational, and physical therapy, our daughter was finally discharged and sent home from the children's rehabilitation hospital.

As we consider all those horrific things that Khalilah had been through in the first six years of her life, it is truly a miracle that she is alive today. If we really think about it, she has survived two comas, one brain surgery, meningitis, respiratory arrest, cardiac arrest, tracheostomy, eye surgery, muscle biopsy, multiple grand mal seizures, pneumonia, and possible covid. It is nothing but the grace of our merciful heavenly Father that has preserved her to this day.

Mentally and physically, she has challenges that will remain with her throughout her life, such as impaired balance and coordination, behavioral, learning, and intellectual deficits.

On the other hand, spiritually, she is perfectly well. She knows what she believes and who she believes in. Her hope is in the soon-coming Savior, at which time she will be fully restored. She is an incentive for us to remain faithful and steadfast, so as a family, my wife, myself, my son, and her will enjoy eternity together.

As devastating as it was, when adversity unexpectedly knocked on my door, though rough and trying, it literally brought Cynthia and I closer together and closer to God. It taught us to put our complete trust in God because He cares for us. And even though bad things may happen to good people, we are confident that there is a God-ordained reason for it. We may not get to understand all there is to know about it in this life, but in God's time, we will get to know it all and love Him even more because of it.

> As devastating as it was, when adversity unexpectedly knocked on my door, though rough and trying, it literally brought Cynthia and I closer together and closer to God. It taught us to put our complete trust in God because He cares for us.

Friends, should the cruel hands of adversity knocked on your door, remember that God will never leave you or forsake you. He has given you the privilege to experience the incredible power of prayer. "Why should the sons and daughters of God be reluctant to pray, when prayer is the key in the hand of faith to unlock heaven's storehouse, where are treasured the boundless resources of Omnipotence?" (White, *Steps to Christ*, p. 94).

> Friends, should the cruel hands of adversity knocked on your door, remember that God will never leave you or forsake you.

We found comfort in the Scriptures. "But the God of all grace, who hath called us unto his eternal glory by Christ Jesus, after that ye have suffered a while, make you perfect, stablish, strengthen, settle you" (1 Peter 5:10). "It is good for me that I have been afflicted; that I might learn thy statutes" (Ps. 119:71). Thank God for the miracle that followed the affliction that came knocking at my door.

Chapter Twenty-Six

The Seventh Miracle at the Last Door

The Door That Changed the World

October 31, 1970 marked the first time that I experienced the celebration of Halloween. Prior to moving to the United States, I was totally unaware that such a thing as Halloween existed, so that October night when I saw young children dressed up in their ghostly attires knocking from door to door shouting, "Trick or treat," I was alarmingly surprised.

But there is another October 31 that has made an even more indelible mark on my memory: October 31, 1517. That was the historic date when Martin Luther nailed his "95 Theses" to the door of the Wittenberg Castle Church over 500 years ago. That anniversary is celebrated as Reformation Day. It commemorates the gallant act of one intrepid man that ignited a flame, known throughout the world as the Protestant Reformation.

The world might have continued the way it was had it not been for the nailing of those ninety-five theses on that door. What if he hadn't followed his deep conviction? Perhaps you and I would not be enjoying religious freedom had it not been for what he nailed to that door.

I believe that Martin Luther was one of the greatest literature evangelists of all times. That one act at the door of the Wittenberg Castle Church in Germany on October 31, 1517, in my estimation, was a miracle at the door and a catalyst that helped to change the world from the dark ages of religious persecution to where we are today.

In one of the books that some literature evangelists carry, *The Great Controversy*, fifty pages are devoted to this zealous, ardent, and devoted man, Martin Luther. He was a man who stood firm on the principles of the Word of God and could not be forced or persuaded against his conscience. Because of his adamant refusal to recant, Pope Leo X excommunicated him on January 3, 1521.

Revelation 13:11–18 warns us of an impending movement that will create a global mandate on how and when to worship God. Those who refuse and choose to worship according to the dictates of their conscience will, like Martin Luther, face the fearsome wrath of the power of church and state. They will be denied the right to buy or sell and even face the penalty of death. However, like Martin Luther, there will be fearless, unwavering, and uncompromising saints of God, who will be willing to say, "Here I stand."

While there is still freedom of religion, freedom of worship, and the exercise of the liberty of conscience, I want it to be said of me, "Here is the patience of the saints: here are they that keep the commandments of God, and the faith of Jesus" (Rev. 14:12).

Thank God for sending Martin Luther to that door of that castle church in Wittenberg, Germany! It was a true miracle at the door.

Chapter Twenty-Seven

The Last Miracle at the Last Door

Not far from the same area where I met the gunman at the door and the couple who thought that I was a Jehovah Witness, I knocked on the door of another man by the name of Henry Crocket.

He was a notable, tall gentleman with an extremely polite disposition. As I explained my mission, he invited me into his home without hesitation. As I sat and conversed with him, I was impressed to show him the medical books, but it seemed that he wanted someone to talk to, so I sat and listened to him as he talked.

In the midst of our conversation, he began to tell me his life story. He started crying while talking about the goodness of the Lord, where the Lord had led him in life and all the various things that had happened to him.

How His Wife Died

He put his finger on the side of his forehead on a conspicuous indentation and began to explain the reason for it. He told me that he and his wife were passengers on an airplane when suddenly, before he knew it, the airplane hit the ground. When he came to himself, he realized the harsh reality that his wife did not survive. The indentation on the side of his head was the injury that he sustained during the crash.

He said that he didn't understand why the good Lord allowed his wife to die but spared his life. His only conclusion is that God perhaps had a purpose in store for him. I was truly moved by his testimony and assured him of the love, goodness, and mercy of the Lord Jesus Christ in saving his life. I also told him that we may not be able to understand why God allows bad thing to happen to good people, but in His wisdom, He has good reason for allowing even bad things to happen to us.

How His Brother Died

Then he began to share another story with me that absolutely blew my mind. He said that God told one of his brothers the day and hour that he would die. I asked him if it happened that way, and he affirmed that his brother died on the same day and hour that he said he would. Then he said to me that he wished that he could die the same way his brother did. After I sat and listened to him at length, his thoughts finally returned to the books. He said he liked the medical books and would like to purchase them.

I Cannot Read

As I was writing up the order, he said something that shocked me. He said that he wanted to let me know that he could not read, but he will buy those beautiful books anyway. At that point, I thought that he was just getting them because I was thoughtful and caring. While thinking about what he said, a thought instantly popped into my mind, and I was impressed to tell him not to worry about it.

By faith, I confidently promised him that I was going to arrange for someone to come and read the books to him. Not only would they read the medical books but they would also read the Bible to him. He was very thankful and asked whether I could really find such a person. He seemed doubtful that there would be someone who would have the patience to come to his home and read to him.

That being said, by faith, I went to the Bible worker of my church, Sister Roberta Davis. She was the paragon of humility, kindness, and willingness, not to mention her winsome personality. When I told her of Mr. Crocket and how he could not read and was not ashamed to have someone read to him, she was moved with compassion and immediately agreed to take on the challenge. Occasionally, when passing by his home to pick up a payment on the books, there she was, patiently and faithfully reading the medical books to him, followed by a Bible study.

His Baptism

As the Bible study continued, Mr. Crocket became so impressed with Roberta and the whole situation that he expressed the desire to join the church to which we belonged. I did not have a form of transportation at the time, but Roberta did, so she volunteered and picked him up every Sabbath morning and took him to church. Finally, at the completion of the Bible study, Mr. Crocket was baptized and became a faithful member of my church.

One of the memorable things about Brother Crocket was how he loved to share testimonies. It was always a joy to listen to him as he stood up in church to testify. Many times, while sharing his testimonies, he would break down in tears in appreciation of God's loving kindness toward him.

He was well up in age and had medical challenges, and as a result, there were times when he would be absent from church. At that point, the church became concerned as it became noticeable that our faithful brother had not attended for a few weeks.

The Sabbath He Died

It was the last month of the quarter, and the church was serving communion that Sabbath. As our custom, our elders, deacons, and deaconesses would team up and visit the sick and shut-ins and serve them communion.

At that time, I was serving as the head elder of my church, and one of my responsibilities was to assign the elders and deacons as to who they would visit and serve communion. That Sabbath I was impressed to ask our pastor, John Wright, to accompany the elders, deacons, and deaconesses who were assigned to serve communion to Brother Crocket.

When they arrived at his home, Brother Crocket gladly received them and cheerfully took communion. After he had finished partaking, he stood up as usual, sang one of his favorite hymns, and gave a testimony. However, on that occasion, he did something that shocked everyone.

First, he told the group the very same story that he had told me the night when I first met him. He told how the Lord revealed to one of his brothers the very day and hour that he would die. And that his brother did die the same day and the same hour that the Lord told him. Then came the shocker. After saying all of that, Brother Crocket stood up and said, "I wish that the good Lord would allow me to die just like he allowed my brother to die."

Then unexpectedly, beyond one's wildest imagination, the most unusual thing happened. Right there, in the presence of Pastor John Wright, an elder, a deacon, and a deaconess, Brother Crocket sat down in his chair and died that very moment on that Sabbath afternoon. That was the strangest of all experiences. It was a stunning and unimaginable shock. Can you imagine that? Someone asked God to let them die, and then God answered the prayer instantly as requested!

At His Funeral

At his funeral service, I met one of his brothers, who was also a Seventh-day Adventist. After the service, he greeted me and asked if I was the literature evangelist who had sold his brother the books which led him to the church. He explained how for years he had been praying for his brother Henry, that God would send someone to witness to him about the Sabbath truth. He was very excited and thankful to God that his prayers were finally answered.

In retrospect, I believe that the night when I met Henry, it was the Lord who impressed me to tell him that someone would come and read the Bible and the medical books to him. I said it in faith, and God honored my faith by providing the Bible worker. "Now faith is the substance of things hoped for, the evidence of things not seen. For by it the elders obtained a good report. ...But without faith it is impossible to please him: for he that cometh to God must believe that he is, and that he is a rewarder of them that diligently seek him" (Heb. 11:1, 2, 6).

Brother Crocket was a praying man with an unflinching faith that God would answer his final prayer request. And God did not hesitate to do so and surely granted his request to die as he uttered it with his final breath.

I believe with all my heart that I will see Brother Henry Crocket when he comes up in the first resurrection, and I want to be there to personally greet him. One day soon, we will all have the opportunity to meet and converse with some of these wonderful people in the kingdom of God. Can you imagine the joy that will burst forth from precious souls when they meet and recognize people who, because of their unselfish efforts and labor with Christ, was the reason for their salvation? What a glorious day that will be!

Chapter Twenty-Eight

A Door of Opportunity for Everyone to Share the Gospel

Is there anything wrong about sharing our faith? How could sharing information of what we believe be wrong when that's what Jesus and all the apostles did?

Furthermore, Jesus commissioned His believers to go and preach, teach and baptize. Matthew 28:19. He also said, "And the lord said to the servant, Go out into the highways and hedges, and compel them to come in, that my house may be filled" (Luke 14:23).

"But sanctify the Lord God in your hearts: and be ready always to give an answer to every man that asketh you a reason of the hope that is in you with meekness and fear" (1 Peter 3:15).

This is an open door of opportunity for all to share their faith. While literature evangelism may not be your calling, if you are willing and missionary-minded, the Holy Spirit can equip you in a way that is unique for you personally to be a soul-winner for Jesus.

In reading the book, *A Guide to Discover Your Spiritual Gifts*, authored by Pastor Mark A. McCleary, D. Min. and Pastor Terrence D. Griffith, I came across an A-Z list of spiritual gifts that I would like to share. I hope that by going through those gifts, those who have not yet discovered their spiritual gift will, by God's grace, make their discovery.

Discovering Definitions and Scriptures for Spiritual Gifts

A. Administration – The ability that God gives to certain believers to organize and coordinate the Church toward its divinely appointed mission. It includes the ability to plan, launch, and complete ministry-related projects to fulfill the needs of God's cause. (Read Luke 14:28–30; Acts 6:1–7; 1 Corinthians 12:4, 28; Titus 1:5).

B. Apostle – The ability God gives to certain believers to go where He sends them to preach/teach to people the truth about God. These individuals are often sent to areas where culture and language differences might be evident. (Read Romans 1:1; Galatians 1:1; 1 Timothy 1:1; 1 Peter 1:1).

C. Celibacy – The ability God gives to certain believers to abstain from sexual interaction willingly and cheerfully, and to live victoriously overcoming sexual temptations. (Read Matthew 19:11, 12; 1 Corinthians 7:7, 8).

D. Discerning of Spirits – The ability God gives to certain believers to distinguish between truth and error and between the influence of the Holy Spirit and evil spirits. (Read Matthew 16:21–23; Acts 5:1–11; 16:16–18; 1 John 4:1–6).

E. Evangelist – The ability God gives to certain believers to share the gospel with unbelievers in such a way that men and women become Jesus' disciples and responsible members of the Church. (Read Acts 8:5, 6, 26–40; 14:21; Ephesians 4:11–14; 2 Timothy 4:5).

F. Exhortation – The ability God gives to certain believers to minister words of comfort, consolation, and counsel to other believers of the body in such a way that they feel helped. (Read Mark 12:41–44; Romans 12:8; 2 Corinthians 9:2–8).

G. Exorcism – The ability God gives to certain believers to detect and expel demons or evil spirits. (Read Mark 5:1–15; Luke 10:17–20; Acts 8:5–8; 16:16–18).

H. Faith – The ability God gives to certain believers to believe, trust, and hope in His word of promise and to demonstrate confidence and inspire other believers to accept and act on God's will and purposes. (Read Acts 27:21–25; Romans 4:18–21; Hebrews 11).

I. Giving – The ability God gives to certain believers to contribute their material resources to the ministry of the Lord liberally and cheerfully. (Read Mark 12:41–44; Romans 12:8; 2 Corinthians 8:1–7; 9:2–8)

J. Healing – The ability God gives to certain believers to serve as healing mediators for God to cure illness and restore health. There service might be apart from the use of natural or medical professional means. (Read Acts 3:1–10; 5:12–16; 9:32–35; 1 Corinthians 12:9, 28).

K. Helps – The ability God gives to certain believers to use their talents to assist in facilitating practical needs of others and thereby empower them to develop effectiveness in expressing their own spiritual gifts. (Mark 15:40, 41; Luke 8:2, 3; Acts 9:36; Romans 16:1, 2).

L. Hospitality – The ability God gives to certain believers to demonstrate a receptive disposition in various settings by offering meaningful welcome, information, and basic assistance. (Read Acts 16:14, 15; Romans 12:9–13; Hebrews 13:1, 2; 1 Peter 4:9).

M. Intercession – The ability God gives to certain believers to pray compassionately for others and to observe specific answers to their prayers. (Read Acts 12:7–12; 1 Timothy 2:1, 2; Colossians 1:9–12; 4:12; James 5:14–16).

N. Interpretation – The ability God gives to certain believers to interpret tongues and potentially confusing information so that others can understand and be edified. (Read 1 Corinthians 12:10, 30; 14:13, 26–28).

O. Knowledge – The ability God gives to certain believers to discover, analyze, and clarify information which is pertinent to the well-being of the Church. (Read Acts 5:1–11; 1 Corinthians 2:14; 12:8; Colossians 2:2, 3).

P. Leadership – The ability God gives to certain believers to direct and inspire others to minister effectively and is exercised with the attitude of humility. (Read Acts 7:10; 15:7–11; Romans 12:8; 1 Timothy 5:17).

Q. Mercy – The ability God gives to certain believers to comfort or help those who need restoration. A special sensitivity toward persons who need reconciliation and revival. (Read Matthew 25:34–40; Mark 9:41; Luke 10:33–35; Acts 11:28–30).

R. Miracles – The ability God gives to certain believers to perform powerful acts which glorify Him and edify His mission of redemption. (Read Acts 9:36–42; 19:11–20; Romans 15:18, 19; 2 Corinthians 12:12).

S. Missionary – The ability God gives to certain believers to share His mission of salvation cross-culturally, and in areas that might be away from their geographical origin and dark to the light of truth. (Read Acts 8:4; 13:2, 3; Romans 10:15; 1 Corinthians 9:19–23).

T. Pastor – The ability God gives to certain believers to shepherd other believers for their spiritual welfare, through counseling and encouraging believers to walk with Christ and discover and develop their spiritual gifts. (Read John 10:1–18; 1 Timothy 3:1–7; 1 Peter 5:1–3).

U. Prophecy – The ability God gives to certain believers to receive and communicate His message, so that hearers will be challenged to consider and respond in faith and might include predictive content. (Read Luke 7:26, 27; Acts 15:32; 21:9–11; Romans 12:6).

V. Service – The ability God gives to certain believers to engage and assist individuals and groups in fulfilling their needs. The ability to make prudent use of resources to meet those needs in practical ways, without demand for distinction or reward. (Read Acts 6:1–7; Galatians 6:2, 10; Titus 3:14).

W. Teaching – The ability God gives to certain believers to instruct and communicate His word effectively. (Read Acts 18:24–28; 20:20, 21; Ephesians 4:11–14).

X. Tongues – The ability God gives to certain believers to speak another language not previously learned to glorify God and authenticate the message of salvation. (Read Mark 16:17; Acts 2:1–3; 10:44–46; 19:1; 1 Corinthians 14:13–19).

Y. Voluntary Poverty – The ability God gives to certain believers to sacrifice material comfort and or luxury and adopt a simpler lifestyle to serve Him more effectively. (Read Acts 2:44, 45; 4:34–37; 2 Corinthians 6:10; 8:9).

Z. Wisdom – The ability God gives to certain believers to apply knowledge or information for its greater practical benefit and impart wise counsel from God's word. (Read Acts 6:3, 10; 1 Corinthians 2:1–13; James 1:5, 6; 2 Peter 3:15, 16). (McCleary and Griffith, *A Guide to Discover Your Spiritual Gifts*, pp. 19–21).

Chapter Twenty-Nine

Practical Ways That My Family and I Share Our Faith

When I retired from my job in 2019, I pledged to the Lord that I would strive to be happier, healthier, holier, and more spiritually active than ever before in my life. After praying about the matter, the Lord exposed me to more ideas that I could incorporate in my personal ministry efforts.

Door Knob Ministry

If you find yourself too timid to share your faith by knocking on someone's door and speaking with them, then leave a book or pamphlet hanging on their door knob. In that way, you are an active but yet an effective nonverbal literature evangelist.

There are some counties where there may be some restriction, but if it is permissible in your county, why not take advantage of the opportunity before the way is edged up and you are not allowed to share your faith? There was a time when the disciples were forbidden to speak or teach in the name of Jesus (see Acts 4:18). We are living in an uncertain age where things are moving with great rapidity. Since the first case of Covid-19 was diagnosed in China, its infection has become the number one issue in the world.

Because of new and unexpected pestilences, the enactment of new legislations, restricting freedom of liberty, freedom of speech, and freedom

> "Because of new and unexpected pestilences, the enactment of new legislations, restricting freedom of liberty, freedom of speech, and freedom of choice may very well soon affect the way we share our faith."

of choice may very well soon affect the way we share our faith. We should not be surprised then how imminent the time is when believers may be fined or imprisoned if they share their faith about Jesus. History will repeat itself (see Acts 5:18–42).

My family and I have placed thousands of free books on door knobs in and around our neighborhood. This has been our Sabbath afternoon personal ministry activity in which we take absolute delight. Free books are supplied to us by a wonderful Christian brother, Roy Dennis, who is serious about sharing the everlasting gospel of the three angel's messages in Revelation 14. He sends out free books by the thousands all over the country and across the world as well.

Lawn Sign

During election time, the majority of front lawns on my street are usually filled with signs displaying people's favorite choices of political candidates. The idea came to me to place a sign on my front lawn declaring my family's candidacy for heaven. On the top of the sign is a logo of the three angels with the verse Revelation 14:6–12 and a caption describing the true values of my household. I also included a number for people to call if they were in need of prayer or curious about Bible studies. Here is the picture of the sign that I placed on my lawn.

The Silent Literature Evangelist

This book rack was set on the front of my home. I call it the silent literature evangelist. Silently, it sits there on a chair for all who walk by to see and take their choice of free literature.

Practical Ways That My Family and I Share Our Faith

Flyers

The supermarkets do it. Pizza shops do it. Contractors do it. AARP does it. Medical institutions do it. So, why can't you send a flyer in your community informing them of your church ministries and services available to them?

Letters

If you are shy in speaking to your neighbor about your faith, you can always drop them a card or letter. Companies and various institutions flood our mail slots with junk mail trying to get our response. So, why can't we send out letters to our neighbors and friends?

Telephone Ministry

Telemarketers are not afraid to call our telephone for solicitation. So why can't we use the telephone to minister to others?

Long before Facebook, Zoom, and social media became a ubiquitous part of the international culture, the telephone was always available.

In January of 2004, Marcia, one of my sisters, who lived in London, had an interest to have Bible studies and asked if I would study with her. I was delighted and studied with her by telephone faithfully every Sunday by long distance. When the study was over, she decided that she wanted to be baptized. So, on her birthday December 18th, 2004, she was baptized by the pastor of the Fulham Seventh-day Adventist Church in London, England.

I have conducted Bible studies with individuals from various cities, states, and countries by telephone that have resulted in a number of baptisms. God gave us the telephone not only for secular use but for His glory as well.

Bible Study on Facebook Messenger

In 2018, I conducted a Bible study with Joy Hinds-Strachan in Edmonton, Canada.

The Bible study was for her, but there were times when she invited friends who occasionally joined in on the study from Canada and from the Islands. Joy was already a believer in Christ. She was a very devoted Christian and was very active in her church ministry. She lived up to all the truth that she knew, but after being convicted on the importance of the Sabbath, she wanted to learn more of what the Bible had to say.

During the course of the Bible study, she learned that the Sabbath was not made for the Jews, but was made for man (see Mark 2:27). She also learned that in the earth made new, people of all nations will continue to worship God on the Sabbath. Her decision and commitment were to follow her conviction and follow where God led even if it meant cutting ties with her former church.

On November 10, 2018, Joy became a new member of the Edmonton North Seventh-day Adventist Church under the leadership of Pastor Keith Samuels.

The Power of Home Bible Study Groups

During the late 1990s, our pastor, Mark McCleary, began to energize the Southwest Philadelphia Adventist Church with the vision of expanding their ministries through spiritual renewal and community-based programs to meet the need of the surrounding area. For many members who were not living in proximity to the church, a program was also designed to help their spiritual needs especially for Wednesday night prayer meeting. As a result, the idea of formation groups was conceived. Each group would meet at the various homes for Wednesday evening prayer meeting.

On April 15, 1998, my family and I volunteered our home as a meeting place for one of such groups to conduct prayer meetings. As the home prayer meeting continued, the number in attendance tripled from eleven to sometimes thirty or more. Because of the notable influx of visitors from the community, the prayer meeting evolved into Wednesday night Bible study hour. As a result, the Lord blessed the efforts with multiple baptisms.

At one point my home became a temporary place of worship. By then, the group had grown and became a newly-formed church known as the Overbrook Park Seventh-day Adventist Company. When we finally moved out to a church building, God had added seven new souls by baptism.

Social Media—A Fulfillment of Bible Prophecy

According the Bible prophecy of Daniel 12, there would be an increase of knowledge in our time. Things that were not understood then would be revealed in our generation. "But thou, O Daniel, shut up the words, and seal the book, even to the time of the end: many shall run to and fro, and knowledge shall be increased" (Dan. 12:4). Through this increase of knowledge, today we can invite thousands through social media platforms to visit our online services.

As you have seen, I have successfully used social media platforms to conduct multiple Bible studies, which resulted in baptisms both in the United States and abroad. God is more than willing to use anyone who is willing to be used.

Personal Invitations

If you are not comfortable writing a note or a letter or do not have access to social media, just extend an invitation to someone to visit your church. We take pride in inviting our family, friends, neighbors, and coworkers to our weddings, our parties, graduations, and multiple other events. Can't we do likewise and invite them to our church with the same degree of enthusiasm?

Results of Personal Invitations

One day while shopping in a department store, I met a very kind and helpful young lady by the name of Vivian, an employee of the store. While talking with her, I was impressed to extend an invitation to her to pay a visit to my church.

Surprisingly, she happily accepted my invitation. That Sabbath when she came to church, she was richly blessed by the worship experience and the warmth and friendly reception of the church. As a result, she requested to take Bible studies. I started to study for a couple of months, but then I turned it over to the Bible worker. After the studies were completed, she was baptized and became a member of God's remnant church.

A Surprising Connection

While riding on the train to work one day, my wife, Cynthia, was impressed to introduce herself to Mr. Allan Gayle, a passenger who was sitting next to her. Although a little timid at first, she eventually started a conversation and extended an invitation to him to visit her church.

On that Sabbath morning when I picked up Allan to take him to church, I was totally flabbergasted when I realized that I actually knew who he was! It so happened that while my daughter was a patient in Thomas Jefferson University Hospital, I was late getting there one night, far past visiting hours, but after I explained my situation to Mr. Gayle, he was very kind to allow entrance. I always appreciated that act of kindness and never forgot it.

During Mr. Gayle's Sabbath visit, the worship experience had a profound effect on him, and he was moved by the Spirit of God to continue visiting. Soon after, he asked for Bible studies. Following his studies, he requested baptism and was baptized by Pastor Mark A. McCleary on March 27, 1993. His loving wife, Miriam, and daughter, Nyoka, later joined the church and became active members as well.

Today, Allan serves as a local elder in the church while his wife plays a very active role in church ministry. What if Cynthia had not heeded the Spirit's prompting to extend that invitation? That is the question.

Block Chaplain

On the block where I live, members gather for occasional block meetings. We have an excellent block captain and treasurer. We also have a block chaplain, which is the role I hold. As the block chaplain, I open each meeting with prayer. I pray for the members of the block, for unity, and the upkeep of our community.

Being the block chaplain, I make myself available when there is a need for prayer. I have visited neighbors when they were in the hospital, and I have also called on members of my church to assist me in house blessing. All I do is to ask my neighbor whether their homes were ever blessed. If they say no, then we can offer them the opportunity. What an excellent way to get to know your neighbor and build relationships.

Every one of us who can pray should take the opportunity and put a note on the doors of neighbors telling them that we are available to pray for them or for their loved ones who have the need for prayer. As servants of God, we are to administer to the needs of our neighbors as good Samaritans. We are to consecrate our mouth, our hands, and our feet in service for our Lord and Savior Jesus Christ. Why not establish yourself as an active block chaplain today right in the corner where you live?

> **"**
> As servants of God, we are to administer to the needs of our neighbors as good Samaritans. We are to consecrate our mouth, our hands, and our feet in service for our Lord and Savior Jesus Christ.
> **"**

The Influence of Our Life

There is another door of opportunity that every child of God can do as a witness for Christ and that is the influence of our lives. As a Christian, the life we live before our family, friends, neighbors, and coworkers is an open book that speaks volumes. "There is an eloquence far more powerful than the eloquence of words in the quiet, consistent life of a pure, true Christian. What a man is has more influence than what he says" (*The Ministry of Healing*, p. 469).

"For I think that God hath set forth us the apostles last, as it were appointed to death: for we are made a spectacle unto the world, and to angels, and to men." (1 Cor. 4:9).

"So speak ye, and so do, as they that shall be judged by the law of liberty" (James 2:12).

Chapter Thirty

Noah's Ark Was the Only Door of Hope

My heart leaped within me as I stepped out of the van. I prayed and thanked God for granting me the opportunity to reach the object that I had traveled so far to see. There on my left, a huge conspicuous boat-shaped object facing me just as clear and distinct as in all the pictures I had seen of it prior to my trip. It was the remains of Noah's ark.

In May of 2007, I was on the road between the borders of two sovereign nations, namely Turkey and Iran, 6,460 miles away from my home. I was with a group on a tour to visit the alleged sight of the remains of Noah's ark whose architect was our great, great ancestor, Noah.

So, there we were in our minivan, navigating curves after curves as we ascended higher and higher on this steep and tortuous gravel and dirt road. I was almost afraid to look out the window at the deep precipices and imminent danger that loomed below us should our driver miss his judgment. I must frankly admit that I came to truly respect his driving skills.

As we continued to ascend up and around, here and there another curve, I curiously wondered when we would reach our destination. But then, suddenly, as if out of nowhere, it appeared before us. There it was sitting on the slope just below the visitors' center, the skeletal remains of a huge man-made ship, away from rivers and oceans. It was docked on a slope of one of the rugged mountains of Ararat, thousands of feet above sea level. While there is not a complete consensus that this is the ark from the Bible, I couldn't help but feeling, thinking, and believing that I was standing amongst the remains of that ancient vessel that once was the only door of hope and place of refuge from the judgment of the flood that devastated our little planet earth over 4,000 years ago.

As I stood there experiencing that precious moment in my life's history, heaven bore witness to my presence on this unique mountain. No matter what I had read or heard of it in the past, at that conscious moment, I became a living eyewitness of that great site. This was one of those ineffable moments in one's life when you cannot predict or anticipate how you would feel or react when you go through a once-in-a-lifetime experience. So, for those brief moments in solitude, my thoughts went out to God in gratitude for placing this reality in front of me and dispelling any hint of fiction or myth.

For many, the question is, how did that massive structure get up to that mountain? Let's take a look at how Moses accurately described that event.

"And the flood was forty days upon the earth; and the waters increased, and bare up the ark, and it was lift up above the earth" (Gen. 7:17).

"And the ark rested in the seventh month, on the seventeenth day of the month, upon the mountains of Ararat" (Gen. 8:4).

The story of that event takes us back to about 4,000 years ago, to a pre-flood civilization known as the antediluvians. In Genesis 6, the Holy Scriptures give a very lurid description of that civilization.

> There were giants in the earth in those days; and also, after that, when the sons of God came in unto the daughters of men, and they bare children to them, the same became mighty men which were of old, men of renown. And God saw that the wickedness of man was great in the earth, and that every imagination of the thoughts of his heart was only evil continually. (Gen. 6:4, 5)

One modern-day author describes it this way. "In the days of Noah the overwhelming majority was opposed to the truth and enamored with a tissue of falsehoods. The land was filled with violence. War, crime, murder, was the order of the day. Just so will it be before Christ's second coming" (White, manuscript 1400, 1990).

Jesus Christ Himself described it this way:

> And as it was in the days of Noe, so shall it be also in the days of the Son of man. They did eat, they drank, they married wives, they were given in marriage, until the day that Noah entered into the ark, and the flood came, and destroyed them all. Likewise also as it was in the days

of Lot; they did eat, they drank, they bought, they sold, they planted, they builded; But the same day that Lot went out of Sodom it rained fire and brimstone from heaven, and destroyed them all. Even thus shall it be in the day when the Son of man is revealed. (Luke 17:26–30)

So, Jesus Christ unequivocally affirms that the ark was not an illusion or fiction but an actual historical fact. That unadulterated statement uttered from the mouth of Jesus was the driving force that inspired me to go and see the remains of the ark for myself.

Other than just going to see the ark for my own satisfaction, I also wanted to be able to present a cogent response when reasoning with some people whose skepticism about the ark cast doubt about the authenticity of the Bible. Many of the people that I come across do not believe in Jesus or the Bible. Therefore, showing that archaeology confirms what Moses wrote and what Jesus and His apostles said lends great credence not only to the accuracy and truthfulness of the Bible but also to its infallibility.

The Only Door of Hope

According to Moses, the author of the book of Genesis, the ark had only one door.

"A window shalt thou make to the ark, and in a cubit shalt thou finish it above; and the door of the ark shalt thou set in the side thereof; with lower, second, and third stories shalt thou make it" (Gen. 6:16).

What is it that was so significant about that door on the side of the ark? It was the only avenue of hope and safety that offered an escape from the imminent destruction about which Noah so fervently preached and predicted. All who wanted to enter had the freedom of choice while that door of mercy was opened.

It was a door of miraculous opportunity. "And they that went in, went in male and female of all flesh, as God had commanded him: and the LORD shut him in" (Gen. 7:16). They witnessed with their own eyes the birds and the animals from forest quietly making their way toward the ark and walking through that door. That in itself was a phenomenal miracle. They had time to make their choice, but they willingly turned their backs from the door.

> Had the antediluvians believed the warning, and repented of their evil deeds, the Lord would have turned aside His wrath, as He afterward did from Nineveh. But by their obstinate resistance to the reproofs of

conscience and the warnings of God's prophet, that generation filled up the measure of their iniquity, and became ripe for destruction. (White, *Patriarchs and Prophets*, p. 97)

For seven days after Noah and his family entered the ark, there appeared no sign of the coming storm. During this period their faith was tested. It was a time of triumph to the world without. The apparent delay confirmed them in the belief that Noah's message was a delusion, and that the Flood would never come. (White, *Patriarchs and Prophets*, p. 98)

Sadly, to say, just as those two legendary cities of Sodom and Gomorrah were destroyed by fire and brimstone for their wickedness so also was the entire pre-flood civilization wiped out from the face of the earth by that great cataclysmic deluge. Today, just as the door of mercy was closed for the generation of the antediluvians, another door is about to close for our generation.

Jesus Christ Himself will make that announcement real soon. Here is what He is going to say:

He that is unjust, let him be unjust still: and he which is filthy, let him be filthy still: and he that is righteous, let him be righteous still: and he that is holy, let him be holy still. And, behold, I come quickly; and my reward is with me, to give every man according as his work shall be. (Rev. 22:11, 12)

Another one of my objectives when at the site of the ark was to spend some time alone on the ark itself in prayer. I had taken with me a large prayer list consisting of several pages filled with the names of friends, family members, churches, neighbors, co-workers, etc. I wanted to present the list before God in prayer while I was on the ark. When that moment came and I was left alone, I knelt beside the huge limestone and poured out my heart to my heavenly Father. I presented to Him the prayer list in sincerity and fervently asked God to grant the same grace to all those on the prayer list that Noah had before the flood destroyed the old antediluvian world.

Seven Days Too Late and They Knew Not

Those who knocked on the door of Noah's ark found out that they were seven days too late. Jesus said that they knew not. "For as in the days that were before the flood they were eating and drinking, marrying and giving in marriage, until the day that Noe entered into the ark, and knew not until the flood came, and took them all away; so shall also the coming of the Son of man be" (Matthew 24:38, 39).

What was it that they knew not? They knew not that their probation was closed seven days earlier when the door was shut.

> They gathered in crowds about the ark, deriding its inmates with a daring violence which they had never ventured upon before. But upon the eighth day dark clouds overspread the heavens. There followed the muttering of thunder and the flash of lightning. Soon large drops of rain began to fall. The world had never witnessed anything like this, and the hearts of men were struck with fear. All were secretly inquiring, "Can it be that Noah was in the right, and that the world is doomed to destruction?" (*Patriarchs and Prophets*, p. 98–99)

While many today are looking towards a new era of peace and prosperity, what message does the story of Noah's ark tell to this current generation? The apostle sums it up most poignantly:

> Knowing this first, that there shall come in the last days scoffers, walking after their own lusts, and saying, Where is the promise of his coming? for since the fathers fell asleep, all things continue as they were from the beginning of the creation. For this they willingly are ignorant of, that by the word of God the heavens were of old, and the earth standing out of the water and in the water: whereby the world that then was, being overflowed with water, perished: but the heavens and the earth, which are now, by the same word are kept in store, reserved unto fire against the day of judgment and perdition of ungodly men. (2 Peter 3:3–7)

As I descended Mount Ararat and looked at the ark for the last time, I left there totally convinced that what I saw, what I stood upon, what I prayed upon, was indeed the remains of biblical ark that Noah built. That same ark that showed God's amazing love and grace by offering a door of hope and mercy is offered today through Jesus Christ. He says, "I am the door: by me if any man enter in, he shall be saved, and shall go in and out, and find pasture" (John 10:9).

> **"**
> That same ark that showed God's amazing love and grace by offering a door of hope and mercy is offered today through Jesus Christ.
> **"**

The story of the ten virgins also accentuates the fact that there will two classes of individuals living on the earth at the second coming of Christ. Like in the days of Noah, the wise will enter in and the foolish will be shut out.

"When once the master of the house is risen up, and hath shut to the door, and ye begin to stand without, and to knock at the door, saying, Lord, Lord, open unto us; and he shall answer and say unto you, I know you not whence ye are" (Luke 13:25). "His lord said unto him, Well done, thou good and faithful servant: thou hast been faithful over a few things, I will make thee ruler over many things: enter thou into the joy of thy lord" (Matt. 25:21).

> It is no arbitrary decree on the part of God that excludes the wicked from heaven; they are shut out by their own unfitness for its companionship. The glory of God would be to them a consuming fire. They would welcome destruction, that they might be hidden from the face of Him who died to redeem them. (White, *Steps to Christ*. p. 17)

Today the door of salvation is wide open, and the benefits are eternal. Why not accept the invitation of Jesus and enter in today?

"O Jerusalem, Jerusalem, which killest the prophets, and stonest them that are sent unto thee; how often would I have gathered thy children together, as a hen doth gather her brood under her wings, and ye would not!" (Luke 13:34).

The devastation that happened to the generation living at the time of the great flood was not a secret event. It was witnessed by all those who were taken by the flood and perished by it. On the other hand, only eight people were left behind alive to tell the story, Noah and his family. Friends, think about it, Noah, our great, great ancestor, what if he did not believe and obey the word of God? You and I would not be here today. This story is to help prepare us to experience a true miracle at the door when Jesus comes again.

The Door of Revelation Three

The door of Revelation 3 is the door to our hearts.

Jesus said,

> Behold, I stand at the door, and knock: if any man hears my voice, and open the door, I will come in to him, and will sup with him, and he

with me. To him that overcometh will I grant to sit with me in my throne, even as I also overcame, and am set down with my father in his throne. (Rev. 3:20, 21)

Friends, there is a miracle in the person of Jesus Christ standing at the door of the heart of every human being. He is earnestly knocking, hoping that He will gain an entrance. Will we let Him in? If we do, there will be a wonderful blessing waiting for us. The Scriptures assure us thusly. "Blessed are they that do his commandments, that they may have right to the tree of life, and may enter in through the gates into the city" (Rev. 22:14).

"While it is said, To day if ye will hear his voice, harden not your hearts, as in the provocation" (Heb. 3:15).

CONCLUSION

Friends, thank you so much for accepting my invitation in joining me on this incredible journey of miracles at the door. I sincerely hope that what you have experienced in all those encounters have drawn you into a closer relationship with Jesus.

We may never know how far-reaching our influences have affected the life of others on this side of heaven. But what indescribable joy will gush forth when we meet with saints in the courts of heaven who are there because of the faithful, kind, and loving thoughtfulness put forth on behalf of their salvation.

The Time is Now

For whosoever shall call upon the name of the Lord shall be saved. How then shall they call on him in whom they have not believed? and how shall they believe in him of whom they have not heard? and how shall they hear without a preacher? And how shall they preach, except they be sent? as it is written, How beautiful are the feet of them that preach the gospel of peace, and bring glad tidings of good things! (Rom. 10:13–15)

"Therefore said he unto them, The harvest truly is great, but the labourers are few: pray ye therefore the Lord of the harvest, that he would send forth labourers into his harvest" (Luke 10:2).

"Also I heard the voice of the Lord, saying, Whom shall I send, and who will go for us? Then said I, Here am I; send me" (Isa. 6:8).

Will you go? My sincere hope is to see you in heaven!

Until then, Maranatha!

Brother Devon L. Roberts

BIBLIOGRAPHY

Gray, Jonathan. *Ark of the Covenant*. 3rd ed. Burleigh Heads, Queensland, Australia: Ind Group Pty Ltd, 1997.

Griffith, Terrence D., and Mark A. McCleary. *A Guide to Discover Your Spiritual Gifts*. Independently published, 2011.

Higgins, William A. *They Walk with Angels*. Washington, D.C.: Review and Herald Publishing Association, 1972.

Kloss, Jethro. *The Original Back to Eden*. New York, NY: Benedict Lust Publications, 2015.

Mandino, OG. *The Greatest Salesman in the World*. New York, NY: Bantam Books, 1983.

Moreau, Roger J. *Beware of Angels: Deceptions in the Last Days*. Washington, D.C.: Review and Herald Publishing Association, 1997.

Padron, Bea J. *Experiences of God's Power with Three Hours to Live*. Frederica, DE: Padron Publishing, 2016.

Walker, Norman W. *Fresh Vegetable and Fruit Juices*. Prescott, AZ: Norwalk Press, 1978.

Whealon, John F. *Living the Catholic Faith Today*. Boston, MA: St. Paul Editions, 1986.

White, E. G. *Colporteur Ministry*. Mountain View, CA: Pacific Press Publishing Association, 1953.

White, E. G. *Counsels for the Church*. Nampa, ID: Pacific Press Publishing Association, 1991.

White, E. G. *The Desire of Ages*. Mountain View, CA: Pacific Press Publishing Association, 1898.

White, E. G. *Manuscript Releases, vol. 19 [Nos. 1360-1419]*. Silver Spring, MD: Ellen G. White Estate, 1990.

White, E. G. *The Ministry of Healing*. Mountain View, CA: Pacific Press Publishing Association, 1905.

White, E. G. *Patriarchs and Prophets.* Washington, D.C.: Review and Herald Publishing Association, 1890.

White, Ellen G. *Steps to Christ.* Hagerstown, MD: Review and Herald Publishing Association, 1890.

TEACH Services, Inc.
P U B L I S H I N G

We invite you to view the complete
selection of titles we publish at:
www.TEACHServices.com

We encourage you to write us
with your thoughts about this,
or any other book we publish at:
info@TEACHServices.com

TEACH Services' titles may be purchased in
bulk quantities for educational, fund-raising,
business, or promotional use.
bulksales@TEACHServices.com

Finally, if you are interested in seeing
your own book in print, please contact us at:
publishing@TEACHServices.com
We are happy to review your manuscript at no charge.

www.ingramcontent.com/pod-product-compliance
Lightning Source LLC
Chambersburg PA
CBHW071209160426
43196CB00011B/2232